Kevin Harney has written a winner—refreshing, engaging, practical, and powerful! Kevin has given us an everyday approach to loving and reaching people for Christ, while also helping us to enjoy the process.

—Nancy Grisham, founder,
Livin' Ignited

God spoke pointedly to my life when reading this inspiring book. It is refreshing to see a very practical book that is solidly grounded in Scripture. While being loaded with practical helps, it refrains from presenting a canned or stereotypical model of witness that everyone should follow. Instead, we see different ways of outreach, which individuals could adopt according to their differing personalities, gifts, and circumstances. This book is unique in being amazingly comprehensive, covering many issues that other books on witness miss out on. Clearly, it is the work of a practitioner.

—Ajith Fernando, National Director,
Youth for Christ Sri Lanka

Every person you meet is an eternal soul. That reality alone underscores the tremendous value of a book like this. Organic Outreach for Ordinary People *will equip any believer to share their faith in effective and natural ways. Kevin presents practical illustrations to communicate with all kinds of people and in all kinds of situations. Reading this book will truly encourage you to raise your evangelistic temperature and passionately pursue that which causes angels to sing—even if you don't have the "gift of evangelism."*

—Marilyn Hontz, author, *Shame Lifter* and *Listening for God*

When Kevin Harney writes about evangelism, I want to read and learn. Kevin is not just writing about this theoretically; he's been doing it for years. Kevin removes the guilt and the awkwardness of evangelism and shows us natural ways to express the good news of Jesus with people all around us. Your heart will grow for people as a result of reading this book.

—Dan Kimball, author, *They Like Jesus but Not the Church*

Personal evangelism is not your thing? You don't have the spiritual gift? The whole idea of sharing your faith seems intimidating and unnatural?

Perfect—this book was written for you! Read it, and with every page you'll be more encouraged and equipped to talk to others—in natural ways—about the things that matter most.

—Mark Mittelberg, author,
The Unexpected Adventure and
Becoming a Contagious Christian
(with Bill Hybels)

Too many people think that evangelism is reserved for a handful of specially gifted people. Read this book and you will say, "I believe God can use anyone, including me, to reach out with his love and good news." Practical, well illustrated, and biblical, this is a great tool to help prepare ordinary Christians to share the extraordinary message of Jesus.

—Lee Strobel, author,
The Case for Christ and
The Unexpected Adventure

ORGANIC OUTREACH

for
Ordinary
PEOPLE

Other Books by Kevin Harney

Leadership from the Inside Out

ORGANIC OUTREACH

for
Ordinary
PEOPLE

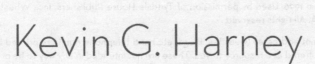

SHARING GOOD NEWS
NATURALLY

Kevin G. Harney

Organic Outreach for Ordinary Families
(forthcoming)

ZONDERVAN.com/
AUTHORTRACKER
follow your favorite authors

ZONDERVAN

Organic Outreach for Ordinary People
Copyright © 2009 by Kevin G. Harney

This title is also available as a Zondervan ebook.
Visit www.zondervan.com/ebooks.

This title is also available in a Zondervan audio edition.
Visit www.zondervan.fm.

Requests for information should be addressed to:

Zondervan, Grand Rapids, Michigan 49530

Library of Congress Cataloging-in-Publication Data

Harney, Kevin.
        Organic outreach for ordinary people : sharing the good news naturally / Kevin
G. Harney.
            p. cm.
        Includes bibliographical references.
        ISBN 978-0-310-27395-0 (softcover)
        1. Witness bearing (Christianity) 2. Spirituality. 3. Spiritual life — Christianity.
I. Title.
BV4520.H373 2009
248'.5 — dc22
                                                                     2009005154

Cover and interior design by Ben Fetterley

Printed in the United States of America

09 10 11 12 13 14 • 23 22 21 20 19 18 17 16 15 14 13 12 11 10 9 8 7 6 5 4 3 2 1

Contents

PART 1

Preparing the Soil

The starting point of effective outreach is not a system, a program, or a specific presentation. It is a heart deeply in love with God and with people. Without love, no outreach strategy will work. With God's love, we can change the world.

If we are going to be effective in sharing the good news of Jesus, we must truly understand and receive the grace of God. Then we can effectively extend God's love to a world filled with people who hunger for a taste of heavenly grace.

The Word of God is true and Jesus is the Truth. As we seek to reach out, we must know what we believe and express it with confidence. God's Word is the source of truth and sound doctrine.

We all have an evangelistic temperature. It can be hot, cold, or somewhere in the middle. It is our responsibility to steward this passion and seek to keep our hearts burning hot and our lives engaged in reaching out.

Evangelism is not a spectator sport. We are all called to get into the game. God invites every follower of Jesus to get off the sidelines and onto the field.

PART 2

Planting and Watering

Prayer is the cornerstone of all effective outreach. We unleash heavenly power when we pray for lost people. We are also called to pray for ourselves and other believers to enter the harvest fields with God's good news.

Praying with unbelievers is an opportunity for God to show up and reveal his power. Organic outreach is propelled forward when we learn to pray with those who are not yet part of God's family.

People need to hear about Jesus, but they also need to see him. As his ambassadors on this earth, we are to reflect his love, show his heart, and incarnate his presence wherever God sends us.

Part of outreach is taking action and having the courage to try new things. There is only one gospel, but there are many ways to express it and to reach people who are spiritually disconnected. Spirit-anointed creativity opens evangelistic doors as we try many ways to scatter the seed of the gospel.

PART 3

Bearing Kingdom Fruit

Acknowledgments

I extend special thanks to the people who had the greatest impact on my seeing Jesus, hearing the gospel, and receiving him as my Savior and the leader of my life almost thirty years ago:

To my sister Gretchen: You endured my small-minded meanness and youthful anger as you loved and served me in the name of a Jesus I didn't know. You met Jesus first, and I am so grateful that you wanted me to know him too. I am glad you are my sister, both by blood and by faith.

To my first pastor, Dan Webster: You preached Jesus with boldness, clarity, and passion. Through your ministry, I not only met Jesus but also heard his call to a life of Christian service.

To the leaders on the Sonshine Ministry houseboat, Gary Webster and Doug Fields: You extended the offer of a new life in Jesus. Thank you for your faithful service and for helping me meet the Savior.

To my friend Doug Drainville: Your example of humble service and tenacious love for God has marked me for a lifetime. Many people spoke to me about Jesus; you showed me he was real through your life.

I also thank those who have been partners in developing and publishing this book:

To my wife, Sherry: Thanks for reading every word and giving your wise input. You make everything I write better.

To my editor Paul Engle: Your partnership over the years continues to bless and inspire me.

To my editor Ryan Pazdur: Your insight and wisdom helped shape the content and flow of this book.

To my editor Brian Phipps: Your eye for detail and sharp mind give me confidence that my work will be cleaner and make more sense after you have done your editorial magic.
To the whole Zondervan team: Thanks for believing in me and for being a partner in ministry for close to two decades.

Introduction

Organic Outreach for Ordinary People

I once saw a woman come up to her friend and say, "Smell my hair."

It seemed like a strange request. But to my surprise, the other woman leaned over and took a big whiff. This led to an extensive conversation about a particular hair-care product. They chatted for a good ten minutes about it. The first woman touted the benefits of her new shampoo with great enthusiasm and passion. The second listened, asked probing questions, and seemed quite intrigued. I don't know if she actually converted to this new wonder shampoo, but her friend's enthusiasm certainly impacted her.

Once, while on a mission trip in the Netherlands, I witnessed another moment of evangelistic fervor. A delightful family was hosting our whole team for dinner. After the meal, a couple of people approached me and said, "You have to try the massage chair!" During the past hour, various members of the group had spent time nestled in a huge black contraption that vibrated and jiggled them. They moaned and groaned as the rollers worked their way up and down their backs, legs, and arms.

Those who had experienced the massage chair were doing all they could to proselytize the rest of us. I did not feel like experiencing the chair, but they were persistent. "You will love the chair! It's amazing! It doesn't hurt. Just try it. It's fun!" I continued in my resolve, but they persisted in doing all they could to get me in the chair, short of picking me up and putting me in it.

We evangelize all the time. When we try a new restaurant that has amazing food, we want others to experience it. We'll even take them out and pay the bill so they can enjoy our discovery. Many people are so enthusiastic about a sports team that they wear clothes that bear the team's name and logo. They memorize players' stats and talk about "their team."

The truth is, when we are zealous about something, when we really love it, we talk about it. We invite others to experience it. We want to share the joy.

Why is it that we can be more enthusiastic about a massage chair or a new restaurant than we are about Jesus? How is it that we can talk naturally about a hair-care product or a sports team, but when it comes to the most important thing in our lives—our faith—we clam up?

It's time for Christians to learn that we can share our passion for God naturally!

But I'm Not an Evangelist

I've lost count of the number of times I have talked with deeply committed and sincere Christians who say, "But I'm not an evangelist." They are quick to say that evangelism is not their gift.

The truth is, the vast majority of Christians don't have the spiritual gift of evangelism. But we are all called to let our lights shine (Matt. 5:16). Every follower of Jesus should let the presence and grace of God illuminate their life. Just because we don't have the spiritual gift of evangelism does not exempt us from reaching out and sharing God's love.

I think about it this way. Some people have the spiritual gift of giving (1 Cor. 13:3). They are generous beyond the norm and share their resources freely. It comes naturally to them. But *all* Christians are called to give with generous hearts and to make their resources available to God (2 Cor. 9:7). We can't say, "I don't have the gift of giving, so it's okay for me to live a selfish and stingy life."

Other followers of Jesus have the God-given gift of compassion (Rom. 12:8). They feel at a deeper level, care authentically, and naturally come alongside people in times of pain, loss, and need. These people minister the grace of Jesus in powerful ways. Does this mean Christians who don't have this gift are free to be hard-hearted and insensitive? Of course not. We are all called to show tenderness and sensitivity. Some have the gift of compassion, but all believers are called to show mercy.

The same is true of evangelism. Some have the gift and it comes naturally to them. But all of us are called to live salty lives that cause others to thirst for Jesus' living water. Every follower of Jesus should reflect God's light so that others will see Jesus' glory. Every person who names Christ as Lord should "be prepared to give an answer to everyone who asks you to give the reason for the hope that you have" (1 Peter 3:15).

The question is not, "Am I an evangelist?" The question is, "Am I a Christian?" When we say, "I follow Jesus," we enter into a whole new way of life. We are called to be generous. We are expected to minister compassion. And the Spirit of God calls each one of us to enter into the challenging and rewarding ministry of evangelism.

Be encouraged! You really can reach out and share the good news about Jesus naturally. Whether you've been talking about your favorite shampoo, that restaurant you love, or your favorite sports teams, you've been practicing already. Now it's time to learn how to share your faith in a natural way. It's time to begin organic outreach.

Organic Outreach for Ordinary People

This book is called *Organic Outreach for Ordinary People*. But what does that really mean?

ORGANIC

When it comes to evangelism, some approaches seem contrived and even manipulative. That is why so many Christians run away from it. It's also why some non-Christians have a negative view of evangelism. The *e*-word has become so tainted that I made a point of not using it in the title of this book! I realized that some Christians might not pick up a book with the word *evangelism* on the cover because the word fills their minds with images of heavy-handed, inauthentic, and coercive tactics. That is not what this book is about.[1]

Organic outreach is about living the kind of life that *naturally* draws people to Jesus. It involves speaking the kinds of words that you use in ordinary conversations and that reveal the presence of a loving God. It means loving people in a way that is genuine. Organic outreach is all about sharing our faith in a way that is authentic, real, and feels natural to the people around us.

OUTREACH

We can call it sharing God's love, bringing the gospel to the world, connecting the spiritually disconnected, doing evangelism, or reaching the lost, but the point is the same. This book is about outreach: how Christians can live and communicate their faith in a way that lets people know there is a God who loves them and sent his only Son to open the door for a restored and wonderful relationship with them (John 3:16). Human beings are lost because of sin, and we need Jesus Christ if we are going to be forgiven, be set free, and find meaning in this life.

Outreach is more than just the proclamation of biblical truth, though this is an important part of the process. It is also about loving people, serving in our community, being models of Christ's grace, building authentic friendships with those who are far from God, and telling our stories of God's presence and power. In this book, we will see that outreach is not just an occasional church field trip to visit those who are spiritually disconnected from God; it's a lifelong journey as we follow Jesus into the world.

ORDINARY PEOPLE

Ordinary people—that's me and you! Outreach is not reserved for the superspiritual, the velvet-tongued, and the hyperextroverted. It's for everyone. We are all called to let the light of Jesus shine in this dark world. Jesus is the living water, and you and I are called to let people know that the soul-quenching refreshment they long for can be found in him alone.

People have asked me, "What kind of person does outreach best?" I tell them that outreach is best done by extroverts, introverts, and everyone in between. It's best done by people who lead with their feelings, by those who approach life with an intellectual bent, and by everyone in between. It's most effective when it's done by the bold and bossy, by the shy and sensitive, and by everyone in between; by those who are longtime mature followers of Jesus, by brand-new believers, and ... you get the point.

Look in the mirror. The person you see is exactly the kind of person God wants to use to bring his love and grace and the message of his Son to the world. The best person to do outreach is an ordinary person just like you. There are people in your community who will be reached best by someone with your temperament, education, personality, experiences, and spiritual heritage. God made you for such a time as this. There are people the Holy Spirit wants to reach out and touch through (take a deep breath) you!

This book focuses on organic outreach for ordinary people. It is about discovering natural ways for regular, ordinary people to share God's love, grace, and message. You can do all of this right where God has placed you in a way that fits exactly how God has wired you.

My desire is that you will find this book to be hope-filled, optimistic, and practical. I don't spend much of my time critiquing outreach methods and programs. The truth is almost any approach to evangelism, if it is rooted in Scripture, done in love, and propelled by the leading of the Holy Spirit, will be fruitful. We are wise to learn from anyone who seeks to bring God's good news to the world. In this book we'll focus our attention on becoming people who are ready to bear and share the good news of Jesus.

I have presented the concepts in this book to tens of thousands of Christians from a vast array of backgrounds in numerous states and countries. I commonly hear comments like these:

"Wow! This makes sense."

"Why didn't someone tell me this stuff years ago? It seems so simple."

"Can it be this easy?"

"Outreach can be fun and natural. Who knew?"

"I can do that!"

Organic Outreach for Ordinary People is not a system or program. It is a collection of simple and biblical practices that Christians everywhere can incorporate into their lives. Open yourself to the leading of the Holy Spirit and watch what God will do in and through you, for his glory and for the good of the world.

Part 1

Preparing the Soil

I didn't see it coming as I walked down the hall of the retirement home. We had just finished visiting some dear elderly people and leading a worship service. The team of volunteers was already out the door, and I was saying my farewells and getting ready to go home. As I walked down the hallway, I noticed an elderly woman sitting by herself in a wheelchair just outside the door of her room. I made eye contact. We smiled at each other. And suddenly, as I walked past her chair, her hand darted out and grabbed mine.

I stopped in my tracks, startled by how quickly the woman had reached out and taken my hand. I had been moving rather quickly and almost could have pulled her arm right out of the socket. She was squeezing my hand with all her might, and I slowly turned and looked at her.

She smiled at me with a longing in her eyes, but didn't say a word. Her frail hand clasped mine in a vise grip, and her piercing eyes stayed locked on mine.

"Hi, I'm Kevin."

She smiled.

"How are you doing today?"

A nod and a bigger smile.

As I stood hand in hand with her, we just looked at each other and shared a moment. In my heart I knew that she desperately needed someone simply to hold her hand, so I did.

After a time, she let go, and her eyes said what her lips could no longer communicate: "Thank you!" I spoke a brief word of blessing and headed out into the afternoon sunlight. When I glanced back, I could see her slight figure sitting in her wheelchair, and I wondered how long it would be before she held another hand.

I have thought of that woman many times since that day. She has become a picture for me of the many people in this world who need a moment of compassion, a smile, an act of grace, or just a hand to hold. And I've thought of the countless people who lack the courage or the speedy reflexes needed to reach out and grab a hand as the world races past.

Many people will never reach out and take our hand, no matter how much they might want to. They need us to stop and extend a hand to them. They need the touch of compassion that God wants to offer through the hands and hearts of his people. When Jesus saw the crowds, he had compassion on them (Matt. 9:36). He saw the people as they really were, sheep without a shepherd. They were unprotected, wandering, in danger. And he cared for them.

This is the kind of heart that should beat in the chests of all who follow Jesus—a heart filled with compassion. And we should have eyes ready to see the needs all around us, hands extended in mercy and service, lips ready to speak words of life. As we walk through this world, some will reach out and grab our hand, while others will need us to reach out to them. In the name of Jesus, we can prepare the soil of our hearts to engage in the most glorious enterprise in all of life: reaching out with God's love and grace.

Every spring my wife, Sherry, plants beautiful flowers—red, pink, white, and purple—in the window boxes in front of our house. They grow and flourish throughout the summer and until the end of fall. I've watched her plant them, and the process is the same every year. She always starts with fresh soil that she carefully places, with her hands, into the boxes. She knows that without good soil, everything she plants will die.

It's a dirty process, and the soil is not all that attractive. But Sherry knows that the life of each plant—its health, growth, and beauty—is dependent on the quality of the soil. The same is true with outreach: the soil must be prepared.

CHAPTER 1

The Law of LOVE

The starting point of effective outreach is not a system, a program, or a specific presentation. It is a heart deeply in love with God and with people. Without love, no outreach strategy will work. With God's love, we can change the world.

" 'Love the Lord your God with all your heart and with all your soul and with all your mind.' This is the first and greatest commandment. And the second is like it: 'Love your neighbor as yourself.' All the Law and the Prophets hang on these two commandments."

—Matthew 22:37–40

"For God so loved the world that he gave his one and only Son, that whoever believes in him shall not perish but have eternal life. For God did not send his Son into the world to condemn the world, but to save the world through him."

—John 3:16–17

One's life is usually about as wide as one's love.

—Philip Hallie

There is a careless streak in love.... It is risky to put oneself out for another, to go out of one's way to help another person—when one is not sure of how to do it well. One may be misunderstood, deceived, hurt. We could flub our overtures of love and end up looking ridiculous. Moved by love, however, we overpower our fear and take the risk.

—Lewis Smedes,
Love within Limits

S ometimes I fiddle around with my wedding ring. I used to play with it more, but I have learned my lesson. For the most part. I was in a movie theater watching a show with some friends. I had taken my ring off. I wasn't really thinking about what I was doing as I moved the ring from finger to finger to thumb, using only one hand. (Try it sometime; it's not as easy as it sounds.)

At one point, while I was moving this precious circle of gold from my pointer finger to my thumb, it popped off and hit the floor. I heard *cling, cling*, and then silence. Then there was another clinging sound, then another. As best as I could figure, the ring had rolled two or three rows down from me.

Now understand, this is not an expensive ring. It has no diamonds. It's a simple gold band. But it's the ring my wife slipped onto my finger on the day we said, "I do." What it lacks in elegance and monetary value, it makes up for in personal significance.

So I slipped out of my chair, in the dark, and moved stealthily down three rows, beginning my search. Have you ever noticed that the floors in movie theaters can be a bit sticky?

I got down on my knees and slowly slid my hands across the floor. Inch by inch and foot by foot my palms slid across the area under the chairs. After about five minutes my hands were stickier than the floor and I still had not found my ring. I moved up a row and started the process all over again.

Thankfully there were no people in the seats as I went through the humbling process of ring searching. Again my hunt was fruitless. Then a thought flashed through my mind. Maybe the ring had slipped into one of the cracks between chairs! I had avoided these areas because they were even more repulsive than the floor. But since my search up to this point was fruitless, I readied my heart, prepared my hands, breathed through my mouth (and not my nose), and upped the ante. I dug between the chairs with my fingers.

I found all kinds of surprises, but no wedding ring.

Now you might wonder, "Why would you crawl on a theater floor and search between the chairs and all the debris and slime just for a ring?"

The answer is simple. The object of my search was so valuable to me that I would do whatever was needed to find it again. For me, the real value of the ring was not in the gold but in its significance as a sign of my love for my wife. That love mattered so much to me that I willingly pressed my fingers into the goop between the legs of the theater chairs.

Love Demands a Search

Love brought God from heaven to earth. Love moved Jesus to empty himself and take on human flesh. Love allowed nails to be driven into the hands and feet of the perfect and pure Son of God. God's love for broken and sinful people is one of the most amazing truths revealed in the Bible. "You see, at just the right time, when we were still powerless, Christ died for the ungodly. Very rarely will anyone die for a righteous man, though for a good man someone might possibly dare to die. But God demonstrates his own love for us in this: While we were still sinners, Christ died for us" (Rom. 5:6–8).

God came searching for us, crawling on the slimy floors of this world. By taking on our sin, he got his hands dirtier than we possibly can know. For some mysterious reason, in God's heart we were worth the cost and humiliation of a search that led from glory to the horror of a Roman cross.

The God who came to seek and save the lost (Luke 19:10) invites us into this same mission. We are not called to make the conversion of unbelievers a project to check off on our list of religious duties. Instead, we are to love people with the love of God. When our hearts beat with the heart of the Father and when a passion for lost people rises up in us, we will be compelled to search and to do all we can to reach out to those who are lost in their sin and are far from God.

Understanding the Law of Love

What motivates us to do the work of evangelism and reach out to spiritually disconnected people?

The desire to carve another notch on our spiritual belts?

A deep sense of guilt or fear?

The need to fill up the seats in our worship center?

None of these are the right motivators.

Many things can drive us toward the work of outreach, but the greatest motivator of all should be love—love for God and love for people. First, our love for God shapes our hearts and makes us more like Jesus. The more we love God and see the world as Jesus does, the more we will move out into the harvest fields. If we want to see outreach become an authentic passion in our hearts, and if we desire to be propelled forward in sharing God's message of life-changing grace, we need to learn to love people the way Jesus does.

To those who asked him what matters most to God, Jesus replied, " 'Love the Lord your God with all your heart and with all your soul and with all your mind.' This is the first and greatest commandment. And the second is like it: 'Love your neighbor as yourself.' All the Law and the Prophets hang on these two commandments" (Matt. 22:37–40).

Loving God and loving others are the two big hooks on which everything hangs. When we think of evangelism, love must be our motivating factor. Jesus made it clear that love is our starting point for everything. Before anything else, organic outreach must be love-driven.

Do I Really Love This Person?

During the question-and-answer period at the end of a session I was leading at an evangelism conference, a man walked up to the microphone and said, "I am trying to reach out to a guy in my neighborhood, but I don't have much in common with him. The truth is, I don't really get along with him all that well." The man explained the tenuous nature of his relationship with his neighbor.

As I listened, I started to feel uncomfortable. This man seemed to see his neighbor as a project, a duty, another item on a spiritual to-do list. But the man was sincere, and I could sense that he really did want to make an impact on his neighbor, so when he finished painting a picture of their relationship, I asked if he would mind answering a question before I responded, and he agreed.

When the question popped out of my mouth, it surprised me, and I had the sense that it caught him off guard as well.

"Do you love him?"

I could tell that he wasn't sure what I meant. So I rephrased the question. "Do you really love your neighbor? Is that what motivates you to reach out to him?"

After a few moments, he answered with humble honesty. "I'm not sure."

What came out of my mouth next did not sound very sensitive, but I meant it with heartfelt sincerity: "I suggest you stay away from him and let someone else reach out to him." I explained that if reaching out was nothing more than a religious homework assignment to him, his neighbor would soon sense his lack of sincerity. His efforts could become counterproductive if they weren't motivated by love.

Since that day, I have reflected deeply on what motivates us to engage in evangelism. I recognize that our motives are never perfectly pure. I am also aware that God can use even wrong motives to accomplish his work of bringing the gospel to the world (Phil. 1:15–18).[2] But the best and most effective driving force for evangelism is sincere love. When the love of God captures our hearts, we are moved by the tender compassion of Jesus. When we see people as lost sheep who need the Good Shepherd (Matt. 9:36), we will naturally reach out to them with hearts that overflow with God's love.

As we respond to the loving mercy and amazing grace of God, outreach happens naturally. When we are loved by God and are passionately in love with the Savior, we desire that others come to know the grace we have experienced.

When we are motivated by guilt or a sense of religious duty, or when lost people become our pet projects, something is wrong. The very people we seek to reach can end up repelled and driven away from the God who loves them. Loving people with God's love is magnetic, attracting people to Jesus. This is organic outreach: evangelism that flows from the love of God.

Growing a Heart of Love

To begin growing a heart of love for those who are lost, broken, and wandering far from God, we can *pray that God will give us a heart like Jesus' heart* toward those who are still living on the borderlands of faith. Pray for God's love to fill your heart to overflowing.

But be warned: this prayer is dangerous.

It's risky to pray this because when we ask God to give us his heart, we know that this is one prayer he is always willing to answer. His love will help us feel on a new and deeper level. Jesus wept over Jerusalem (Luke 19:41). God loves people with absolute desperation. If we have even a small fraction of God's heart for people, tears will flow, compassion will grow, and hearts will break. We will never be the same.

Another way we can grow our heart for those who are spiritually disconnected is to *study the life of Jesus*. As we discover how the Savior related to those who were deep in sin and spiritually lost, we can gain a vision for connecting with others that will shape our hearts and our lifestyle choices. Jesus talked with and let his heart be touched by an adulterous woman (John 8:1–11), a dishonest businessman (Luke 19:1–9), "sinners" (Matt. 9:9–12), and a broken woman (Luke 7:36–50). Jesus' example and his love for people, even the "tough people," can inform our priorities and help reshape our hearts into ones that look a lot like his.

One additional way we can grow a heart for people on the borderlands of faith is to *notice and connect with people who are far from God*. Jesus had a way of seeing the sick, stopping for the broken, making space for children, touching those who had leprosy, and connecting in an authentic way with people many others in the religious community avoided. We can develop a discipline of noticing and making space for those who are spiritually disconnected and often marginalized even by Christians. As you spend time with these people, God will grow new love within you.

As we prepare the soil of our hearts for the work of outreach, it is critical that love rules the day. Love brought God from heaven. Love put Jesus on the cross. Love offered salvation to you and me.

And love will drive us to our knees in prayer and into the world searching for those who are still lost. When we love God and our hearts are captured by his love, we are compelled to reach out to those who are still far from Jesus.

Back to the Theater Floor

So whatever happened to my lost wedding ring? To my delight, after what felt like hours searching for my ring in the darkness, I finally hit gold! Wedged between the legs of two chairs, three rows down from my seat, I found the small band that belonged on the ring finger of my left hand.

After washing the ring, my hands, and the knees of my jeans, I returned my ring to my finger, where it remains to this day. That moment and the feelings associated with it are seared in my mind.

It was worth the search.

God is still reaching into dark places, looking for those who are lost. God is the original seeker. Though we may talk about "spiritual seekers," the truth is that God is always the first and primary seeker. He is the one who left the glory of heaven to come and live among us. And God calls us, as his followers, to get into the business of seeking. We are to join him in searching for those who are lost.

My wedding ring is important to me, but the souls of men, women, and children are infinitely more valuable! Joining God in his search for the lost will mean getting our hands dirty. Crawling around on theater floors is child's play compared with what you and I will face when we join God in his search for those who are spiritually lost. Only God-empowered love can make us willing to reach out like Jesus did. Only the love of God can infuse us with the power and energy we need to keep up the search, even when it feels hopeless.

God got his hands dirty for us. He showed us his love—all the way to the cross. As his love captures our hearts, organic outreach will flow naturally from our lives. And when this happens, congregations and communities will be transformed. Evangelism, fueled by a love for God's glory and the joy of seeing lost people found, will become a natural and unstoppable force.

PREPARING THE SOIL

Organic Activity: I Can Do That!

- *Five Days of Prayer.* Identify one person you know who is far from God. Commit to pray for this person for the next five days. Lift up these two simple prayers: (1) "God, help me love this person the way you do. Give me your heart for them"; (2) "Holy Spirit, please draw this person to yourself. Soften their heart and reveal yourself to them."

- *Jesus Study.* Pick one of the Gospels (Matthew, Mark, Luke, or John) and read a chapter each day, looking for one recurring theme: How did Jesus love people? Seek to learn from the example and teaching of the Savior.

- *Connection Time.* Look at your schedule for the next week and make sure you have some time blocked out for connecting with people who are not believers. If you don't have any time scheduled to be with non-Christians, adjust your schedule.

Personal Reflection

- As I think about the life and example of Jesus, what do I learn about how he loved and cared for those who were lost in sin and far from God?

- Who is one unbelieving person God has placed in my life, and what step can I take to connect more closely with them and allow God to increase my love for them?

Group Reflection

- Describe a time when you felt the love of God capture your heart and you began caring about a lost person because the heart of Jesus was beating in yours.
- Who is one spiritually disconnected person you hope to share the gospel with? Talk about what is motivating you to reach out to this person. How can you grow a deeper love for them?

Prayer Direction

God of heaven, overwhelm me with reminders of your love for me. As I revel in your love, let it overflow to others. If my heart is calloused and insensitive, bring it to life again. Help me love people so much that it involves risk, that my heart breaks, and that I follow you in your mission of reaching the lost. Here I am, ready to crawl through the muck and mire of this world, side by side with you. When it is dark and dirty and I feel ready to give up, let your love compel me to press on. Amen.

CHAPTER 2

Becoming Grace BEARERS

If we are going to be effective in sharing the good news of Jesus, we must truly understand and receive the grace of God. Then we can effectively extend God's love to a world filled with people who hunger for a taste of heavenly grace.

But because of his great love for us, God, who is rich in mercy, made us alive with Christ even when we were dead in transgressions—it is by grace you have been saved. And God raised us up with Christ and seated us with him in the heavenly realms in Christ Jesus, in order that in the coming ages he might show the incomparable riches of his grace, expressed in his kindness to us in Christ Jesus. For it is by grace you have been saved, through faith—and this not from yourselves, it is the gift of God—not by works, so that no one can boast.

—Ephesians 2:4–9

The many uses of the word in English convince me that grace is indeed amazing—truly our last best word. It contains the essence of the gospel as a drop of water can contain the image of the sun. The world thirsts for grace in ways it does not even recognize; little wonder the hymn "Amazing Grace" edged its way to the Top Ten charts two hundred years after its composition. For a society that seems adrift, without moorings, I know of no better place to drop an anchor of faith.

—Philip Yancey,
*What's So Amazing
about Grace?*

J ustice is getting what we deserve.
  Mercy is *not* getting what we deserve.
Grace is getting what we *don't* deserve.
Let me clarify these definitions with a story.

Imagine I have just walked out of a restaurant after a delicious Mexican meal with some friends. The salsa is still on my lips, I feel comfortably full, and the universe seems at peace.

As I walk into the parking lot, I see a young man standing next to my car. He has a set of keys in his hand and there are a series of scratches along the side of my car. It quickly becomes apparent to me that he has "keyed" my car. He has vandalized my VW Jetta by walking alongside it and dragging a couple of keys against the paint. Our eyes lock, his face turns red, and time freezes as flecks of black paint from my car float slowly to the ground. He doesn't run. He just stands there.

As I approach him, all kinds of thoughts and feelings rush through me—he has just defaced my car! When I reach the young man, he begins to apologize. He tells me he is sorry and will pay to fix the damage. In this moment all three concepts—justice, mercy, and grace—come into play.

I can call for justice, making sure he gets what he deserves. At the bare minimum I can take him up on his offer to pay for the repairs. It might even be appropriate to call the police, file a report, and let him stand before a judge.

We all want justice. When someone has wronged us, we are quick to demand vindication and restoration. We believe in justice, we want justice, we even demand justice ... most of the time.

The truth is, we are quick to cry for justice when we have been wronged, but not so swift to demand justice when we are the perpetrator. Consider the moment we hear a siren, look in the rearview mirror, see a flashing red light, and then glance at the speedometer to find that we are driving twenty miles an hour over the speed limit. In the panic of that moment, with the officer asking for our license, most of us aren't going to say, "I demand justice! Whatever you do, please make sure I pay the full penalty for my crime."

At that moment the *last* thing we want is justice. What we really want is mercy. We want the officer to refrain from giving us what we deserve. Instead of wanting justice, our hearts cry for mercy: "Whatever you do, don't give me what I deserve!"

Go back with me to the parking lot of the Mexican restaurant. The smell of salsa is still on my breath, but I am no longer feeling like the universe is at peace. The young man is standing there, keys in hand, paint flecks floating to the ground, tears in his eyes, filled with sorrow, and crying for mercy.

I have a choice. I can demand justice, call the police, and make him pay for his crime. Or I can extend mercy. At this point I might say, "You are free to go," and let him off the hook. Mercy like this doesn't make sense in a world filled with retaliation and compensation for any and all wrongs. Mercy can seem foolish and overly generous. As extravagant and reckless as mercy appears, it is eclipsed by the sheer glory of grace. What could grace look like as I stand face-to-face with this young man who has vandalized my car? Imagine that I look at him, reach into my pocket, take out my keys, and offer them to him. I say, "Here are my keys—the car is yours. It is a gift from me to you. I'll sign over the title. Let me fill the tank up before you go. And if you want to get those scratches fixed, feel free to send me the bill. I'd be glad to pay it!"

This is the realm of grace. Grace is getting what we do not deserve. It is exorbitant, senseless, staggering. Grace takes our breath away and leaves us gasping in stunned amazement.

A God of Grace

In the spiritual realm God deals with the need for justice through the work of Christ on the cross, he shows us mercy by forgiving our sins, and he showers us with grace when we trust him by faith. The wages of sin is death (Rom. 6:23). The price for sin must be paid. Because God is just, he cannot ignore the reality of our sin. Jesus, the sinless Son of God, died in the place of sinful people like you and me (1 Peter 2:24) to satisfy the just judgment of God.

The Father extends mercy by not making *us* pay for our sins. He removes our sins as far as the east is from the west (Ps. 103:12) and frees us from both guilt and judgment. In Christ, we do not get what we deserve. God's mercy is not at the expense of his justice.

Because Christ has been judged in our place, we do not receive what we deserve—punishment for our sins. What hope-filled and amazing news! Mercy is a great gift.

But God's love goes one step farther. God overflows with such amazing grace that he offers us far more than a set of keys to a car. He offers the life of his only Son. He freely extends his love, friendship, and every spiritual blessing in the heavenly realms (Eph. 1:3). The perfect, sinless life of Jesus, lived in obedience to the Father, has been credited to us. "God made him who had no sin to be sin for us, so that in him we might become the righteousness of God" (2 Cor. 5:21). We become living expressions of God's goodness, grace, and glory! The grace of God is so extravagant that it almost appears reckless, defying any logical explanation.

Someone might watch me hand over the keys of my car to a person who has defaced it and think I have lost my mind. I would appear ridiculous and foolish. But our offenses against a holy God are infinitely greater than a few scratches on the side of a car. His offer of grace is infinitely more valuable than a VW Jetta.

If we are to reach out to people in our community and world, we must live each day amazed by the wonder of God's grace. As we reflect on the depth of our sin and remember the height of God's love, our hearts will be powerfully captured by the good news we have for the world.

Amazing Grace

Organic outreach, motivated by love, must be infused with the amazing grace of God. If we don't get this whole grace thing, we will never be effective in the work of evangelism.

Some followers of Jesus seem to be obsessed by the bad news of sin. They want to dwell on the penalty of sin and the reality of hell. As you read this book, you will discover that I wholeheartedly believe that the Bible teaches that all of us have sinned and fallen short of the glory of God. I believe that the consequences of sin are death and eternal punishment for all those who are not saved by the grace of God offered in Christ. But we must always remember that our primary message is not the bad news of hell, but the good news of God's grace offered in Jesus.

We need to embrace two distinct and interlocking aspects of grace if our outreach is going to become organic. First, we must embrace the humbling and profound reality that the God we worship is the author of grace. Grace flows from God and emanates naturally from his heart. No one in the entire universe is more grace-filled than the God of the Bible. It was grace that sent Jesus into this world, and it was grace that held him on a Roman cross. Only grace could have reached out to us in our rebellion and sin and offered us the gift of Jesus. And it is grace that sustains us each day. Every second of life, every breath we take, each sunset, every moment of laughter, each and every good gift in life comes from the God of grace.

If we are going to live lives that organically and naturally reach out to the world, we must enter each day aware of and astounded by the wonder of God's grace. We must begin with a change in our perspective. Can you see the grace-filled eyes of your heavenly Father looking at you as you stand by the car with flecks of paint in the air and keys in your hand? The truth is that we are the vandals; we are the ones who have defaced the holy heart of God. You and I are sinners saved by grace. We deserved hell but have been given something we did not deserve: the love and friendship of God and an eternal home with him in heaven.

It is one thing to acknowledge the theological reality that God is gracious. It is another thing altogether to personally receive that grace and breathe it into your soul each day.

Grace in a Grace-Starved World

None of us have our own reservoir of grace to offer the world. In fact, if we are honest, we must recognize that everything we have is really on loan from the author of grace. When we understand the gracious character of God and live each day with a profound awareness of his love for us, sharing grace becomes natural, reflexive, and — dare I say it? — organic.

As we become bearers of God's grace to the world, the presence of Jesus and the love of God break into history over and over again. Grace bearers are marked by behaviors and attitudes that stand out in this graceless world.

Reckless love is one of the marks of a grace bearer. I will never forget the atmosphere that filled the room when I first walked into the youth center of Garden Grove Community Church almost three decades ago. I had never been in a place filled with high school students who actually loved each other ... and me. It surprised me. It confused me. And it drew me in as my heart longed to be part of a community of people who understood love.

While I was still investigating the Christian faith, my sister Gretchen was a fresh new follower of Jesus. She began to love me with reckless abandon. Our formally combative relationship became confusing for me because she no longer wanted to fight. She was nice to me. To my shame, I cursed her and even threw her Bible on the floor and stomped on it. She retaliated with kindness and assaulted me with love. It was reckless, nonsensical, and exactly what I needed. God used the strong love of my sister to break through my heart of stone. I am eternally grateful.

As God's grace permeates our hearts, love for others will flow. Reckless, dangerous, costly, and authentic love for people is an indicator that we understand God's grace toward us.

Generous forgiveness is another sign that grace is in us and overflowing to others. Jesus had a great deal to say about this (Matt. 6:12–15; 18:21–35). Even a cursory study of the life of Jesus will uncover the fact that he expects his followers to extend forgiveness in the same way he offers it to us. That is setting the bar pretty high, and that's exactly what Jesus wants to do.

If we are going to be grace bearers in this world, we will learn to leverage the moments when we have been wronged, hurt, burned, and abandoned. These become doorways to evangelistic activity. When we forgive, we reveal the presence of a God who brings grace to those who do not deserve it. If we refuse to forgive, we slam the door on a potential Holy Spirit–laden moment. Every time we choose to forgive someone who has wronged us we unleash the very grace that saved us.

Sacrificial sharing is a third indicator that grace has taken up residency in our lives. We bear the grace of Jesus Christ and unleash it in our relationships as we take all we have and hold it in open hands. Sharing is a revelation that God is present and transforming our lives.

My wife, Sherry, is one of the most generous people I have ever met. She will give away everything she can. Her passion for giving is a direct response to her awareness of God's love and grace for her. It is also a natural by-product of her desire for others to taste the goodness of God. Sherry doesn't have to work at being generous; her generosity flows organically from a heart that has been forgiven and filled with God's grace.

Our three sons have gone through the local public schools from kindergarten through high school. All of the teachers, administrators, and office staff know my wife. They love her and she loves them. Through the years she has lavished them with gifts. Most are not expensive or extravagant, but they are always thoughtful. Years ago Sherry told me that she was concerned that though our boys' teachers got gifts at Christmas and on special occasions, the office team and administrators were often forgotten. She wanted to make sure they were remembered on holidays and special occasions. Sherry gives gifts to neighbors, family members, anyone she feels would be blessed by receiving a special gift.

Over the years, some of the recipients of these gifts have told Sherry that her sacrificial giving has been a witness to the presence and grace of God. Since Jesus gave his life freely as a gift to us, we can model his presence and heart when we enter into a ministry of generosity.

Though there are many other markers of a grace-bearing lifestyle, the one I want to conclude with is *a heart open to embrace and engage people who are different.* Some Christians withdraw from the world and retreat to a life cloistered away from everyone who is not part of God's family. Some take this sad pathology a step further and will only associate with their particular brand of Christianity. This was never the way of Jesus, it does not reflect the heart of God, and it certainly fails to communicate his grace to the world.

Jesus was drawn to the outcast and broken people of his day. He was comfortable conversing about spiritual things with a woman who was an outsider in her own town (John 4). Our Savior reached out and touched people afflicted with leprosy, shared meals with tax collectors, interacted with prostitutes, enjoyed connecting with the religious elite, was comfortable with fishermen, and mixed and mingled with every possible class of people.

In the same way, followers of Jesus in our day should be ready to engage with those who might appear different than us. Christians should be comfortable spending time with people who are trapped in sexual addictions and moral lifestyles that are contrary to the teachings of the Bible. We should be drawn to those who are marginalized and forgotten in our culture. From the very rich to the very poor, even if people are vastly different than us, the love of Jesus should draw us to reach out to them. The church is beginning to learn how to reach out and hold the hands of people battling HIV and AIDS. We must continue on this pathway. Like Jesus, we are to engage with and love people from every walk of life.

For those who worry that their integrity and witness might be compromised if they hang out with "questionable folks," it might be helpful to remember the example of Jesus when he interacted with the woman caught in adultery. Jesus expressed love and spoke words of forgiveness, but he was also clear about her lifestyle: "Go now and leave your life of sin" (John 8:11). Jesus had no problem showing love and giving correction to people at the same time.

Jesus also knew that some of those watching from the outside would never understand why he felt so comfortable spending time with "sinners." There would always be those who would accuse him of being a "friend of tax collectors and 'sinners'" (Matt. 11:19). But Jesus wore this label gladly. Maybe it's time for some of us to wear that label too, even if we are accused of hanging with "those kinds of people." What an honor it would be—a sign that our lives are truly captured with a Christlike passion for the lost!

To be prepared for the work of outreach, the soil of our own hearts should first be drenched with the refreshing waters of God's grace. Then, as our hearts overflow with the love of God and his goodness, we become conduits of his grace to the world. Like a man in a desert who is dying from thirst, this world is grace-parched. People are thirsty, dying for a drink that will sustain their dry hearts. We can offer the water that will refresh them.

PREPARING THE SOIL

Organic Activity: I Can Do That!

- *Drink Deeply.* If you are not experiencing grace in your own soul, take time to drink deeply of God's grace for you. Spend time meditating on and memorizing Ephesians 2:4–9. Let the truth of God's grace and love capture your heart anew. Celebrate it. Receive it.
- *Get Reckless.* Think of one extravagant and undeserved act of loving grace you can offer to a person in your life who is not a follower of Jesus. Offer it prayerfully and with no strings attached. If they ask you why you did what you did, tell them about the grace you have received and how it compels you to extend the love of God to others.

Personal Reflection

- How am I doing at receiving the grace God offers me each day? What can I do to open my heart to receive God's grace more fully?
- Who has wronged me and I have refused to forgive them? What can I do to forgive this person (in my heart and actions)?
- Do I tend to avoid certain people or groups of people because I see them as "sinful" or a threat? What can I do to connect with someone who is different from me?

Group Reflection

- Tell about how someone revealed the grace of God to you in one of the following ways:

Through reckless love
Through generous forgiveness
Through sacrificial sharing
Through openheartedness

- Does your church tend to avoid or push away certain kinds of people because they are seen as sinful or unapproachable? How might your group help your congregation reach out to them and extend the grace of God and the love of God's people?

Prayer Direction

God of grace, I have been caught in the act. I have defaced your glory and sinned against you. I am still amazed at your grace. I deserved punishment, but you took my place on the cross. I deserved separation from you, but you embraced me as a loved child. I deserved hell, but you offered heaven through the sacrifice of your only Son. When I get a glimpse of your grace, I am overwhelmed. O God, with a trembling heart I pray, let your grace flow through me. Fill me with so much grace that it cascades from me to everyone I meet each day. For your glory, amen!

CHAPTER 3

Embracing the
Bible and
TRUTH

The Word of God is true and Jesus is the Truth. As
we seek to reach out, we must know what we believe
and express it with confidence. God's Word is the
source of truth and sound doctrine.

For the time will come when men will not put up with sound doctrine. Instead, to suit their own desires, they will gather around them a great number of teachers to say what their itching ears want to hear.

—2 Timothy 4:3

Jesus answered, "I am the way and the truth and the life. No one comes to the Father except through me. If you really knew me, you would know my Father as well. From now on, you do know him and have seen him."

—John 14:6–7

John 14:6 presents a comprehensive case for the uniqueness of Christ. As the Way He is unique, because only through Him and His work can we find salvation. As the Truth He is unique, because He alone is absolute truth. Although other ideologies may have many truths, Jesus is absolute truth. As the Life He opens the way for us to experience life to the full. This is what God made us for, and it is the only completely fulfilling life.

—Ajith Fernando,
*Sharing the Truth
in Love*[3]

When I became a follower of Jesus, I had no spiritual heritage or religious foundation. I grew up in a loving home, but I cannot ever remember seeing a Bible or hearing it read. I had been to church with my family only on a few special occasions, more out of social convention than religious conviction. I was so unchurched that I had no idea Easter and Christmas were religious holidays.

By God's grace, my heart and eyes eventually were opened and I met Jesus. I believed and received him as my forgiver and the leader of my life. I still had lots of questions, but I knew Jesus loved me and had offered his life as a sacrifice for me, to pay for my sins. I received his free gift. I was a new person. I was born again (John 3:3).

After taking this step of faith, I entered into a whole new season of learning and growth. I knew only a little bit about the Bible—the basic gospel. Beyond this I knew that short portion of Luke that Linus quotes in the Charlie Brown Christmas cartoon our family watched on TV every December.

I was a biblical illiterate.

A couple of days after I became a follower of Jesus, one of the volunteer youth leaders from the church gave me an amazing gift. He handed me a Bible. It was a hard back Harper study bible in the Revised Standard Version. His instructions were clear and simple: "Kevin, you are a Christian now. You are supposed to read this every day."

That was my training.

I realize that some will find this approach woefully inadequate, but it worked for me.

A few months later I asked the youth leader who gave me the Bible, "Now what do I do? What do I read next?" He looked at me with a puzzled expression and asked, "How far did you get?" I said, "I'm done." He pondered my response, paused, and then gave me step two in my training regimen: "Read it again!"

For the past thirty years I have been reading the Bible again, and again, and again. This discipline of feasting on the Word of God has shaped my theology and understanding of truth. I might sound like a bit of a caveman to some people, but I don't think things have to be as confusing and convoluted as we often make them. God's Word is truth. Our understanding of reality should be shaped by the clear and powerful teaching of Scripture. When we let the Word of God define our beliefs and form our doctrine, we naturally want to share the good news of God's love with others. When Christians start to get fuzzy on God's Word and compromise on the truth, their passion for outreach wavers and they quickly lose their focus on this high calling.

Doctrine Matters

People in some Christian circles today seem to think we can't confidently know truth. They think doctrine is old-fashioned and confining. They are more comfortable reimagining or repainting the Christian faith. Rather than looking to God's Word and discovering eternal truth that can shape and guide our lives, they seem more interested in dissecting, debunking, and questioning the doctrines and beliefs that have been embraced by Christians for the past two millennia. Core teachings and doctrines of the Christian faith are being treated like a garnish on the side of a plate at a fancy restaurant. Some are suggesting we toss these beliefs out like a sprig of parsley. They serve a decorative purpose but are not essential to our faith.

What these "innovative" and "revolutionary" thinkers fail to recognize is that they are tossing out fundamental beliefs that define the Christian faith. Without these truths intact, we are no longer the church of Jesus Christ. We become a social club of do-gooders who no longer embrace or share the core truths of the Christian faith. But what we believe really does matter! The core, unifying beliefs of the Christian faith have always been founded on the teaching of the inspired written Word of God—the Bible.

Our beliefs matter to God because he is the one who breathed the very words of Scripture (2 Tim. 3:16). Our doctrine matters because what we believe determines how we live, love, and reach out to the world. The core beliefs of Christians are also of interest to those who are not yet believers in Jesus Christ. They are watching us and wondering if we really believe what we say we believe.

Thom Rainer, when he served as the dean of the Billy Graham School of Missions, Evangelism, and Church Growth, wrote a book called *Surprising Insights from the Unchurched*.[4] A brilliant researcher on topics of faith and evangelism, Rainer based his book on interviews and conversations with thousands of unchurched people. In the midst of his research, he discovered one key and surprising insight: our doctrine matters to those who are spiritual seekers. Keep in mind, this research wasn't done in the 1960s or '70s! Rainer wrote his book after the turn of the new millennium. In a day and age when some Christians find talk about absolute truth claims embarrassing and avoid discussions about doctrine, studies like this show that unchurched people really do care about what we believe. They want to know if we actually have convictions about our faith. Rainer reports, "Because almost nine out of ten formally unchurched people told us that doctrine was the major factor in their choosing a church, we delved further into this issue. 'Why,' we asked, 'is doctrine so important to you?' The most frequent response was their desire to know truth or absolutes."[5]

Many "experts" on postmodernism parrot the party line that people today don't believe in truth and absolutes. They even recommend developing "humble uncertainty" about our beliefs as followers of Christ. This approach to life and faith undermines the very teachings of the one who is the Truth. Jesus taught that we should be *humbly certain* about his claims and the faith we profess, passed down from those who have gone before us.

People in the world are looking at you and me and wondering whether we really believe what we say we believe. Are we confident of the truth of God's Word? It's time for followers of Jesus to adopt a posture of certainty about the Bible. We must humbly submit our lives to the teaching of Scripture with confident assurance that it is the very Word of God and our authority for life. Humble? Yes! But also confident that the Word of God is true and our faith will stand up under any and all scrutiny.

The Love of God Revealed in the Sacrifice of Jesus

If we take the Bible seriously, we are faced with some sobering realities. First, God's passionate love is greater than we can comprehend.

The price the Father paid to purchase our forgiveness involved the greatest sacrifice in the history of the world: the life and blood of his only Son, Jesus Christ. The cross, though a brutal and bloody picture, points us to the depth of God's sacrifice and the height of his love for us. God's amazing grace is clearly taught in Scripture; we can never compromise this or toss it aside. To forfeit our belief that the cross of Jesus as the centerpiece of our salvation is to lose the heart of biblical faith.

In recent years, some people in the church have taught that the doctrine of the substitutionary sacrifice of Jesus on the cross is a barbaric idea invented by medieval theologians. Some have actually called the doctrine of the cross a form of divine child abuse.[6] Rather than seeing the cross of Calvary as a picture of God's loving redemption, they suggest that this belief, embraced by the church for two thousand years and taught clearly in the Bible, advocates and perpetuates violence. It makes them uncomfortable. They don't like it. So they sweep it under the carpet and try to rewrite the clear teaching of God's Word.

Yet the Bible clearly teaches that *God* established the sacrificial system and called the priests of the Old Testament era and the people of Israel to follow specific instructions when they brought their offerings. The sacrificial system was a powerful and graphic picture pointing us to the ultimate offering of God's love for us: Jesus crucified for our sins. The sacrificial system was a divinely designed practice foreshadowing God's redemptive plan for his people, brought to fulfillment on the cross by Christ.

The Word of God teaches, without reservation or apology, that the sacrifice of Jesus, as bloody and horrible as it sounds, was necessary to pay for our sins (Rom. 5:8; 1 Cor. 15:3; Heb. 9:15; 1 Peter 3:18; 1 John 4:10). As followers of Jesus, we must cling to this truth as if our lives depend on it — because they do! If we are going to be stirred to engage in the work of outreach, it's mandatory that we have a humble confidence in the sin-bearing work of Jesus. If you find yourself rubbing shoulders with people who bear the name of Jesus yet reject the teaching that Jesus died for our sins in our place, take time to pray for their eyes to be opened to the truth of God's Word.

People Are Lost without Jesus

The Bible teaches that people are lost without Jesus. Many today reject the term *lost* and the idea that people need Jesus for salvation. A creeping universalism is slowly invading some quarters of the church.[7] The notion that all religions are equally valid and lead to salvation has no biblical support.[8]

Others argue that our modern world has so much religious diversity that we must accept the idea that there are many pathways to God. They believe it is arrogant and intolerant to teach that there is only one way to heaven—through Jesus. But in the days of Jesus and the apostle Paul, the Roman world was filled with religious diversity. The religious diversity of our day is not unique; a vast array of spiritual options has always been available to people. In Paul's day there were so many religions that the people created numerous temples for their countless "gods." They even built shrines for "unknown gods"—just in case they missed some (Acts 17:16–23)! The Christian faith has always had rivals and the world has always offered a plethora of religious expressions; the challenges of our day are nothing new. Still the Bible teaches, without apology, that there is only one way to God.

In the Old Testament, the God of Israel clearly taught that his people were to worship him alone. The first two of the Ten Commandments emphasize this call to fidelity in our worship: God alone is to be loved above all else (Exod. 20:2–6). Throughout the Old Testament, the people of Israel were taught that idolatry of any kind was abhorrent and intolerable. The times of Israel's greatest failings came when the people forgot that they were to worship the Lord their God and serve only him. When their hearts wandered to idols and false gods, judgment always followed.

God's desire to be in an exclusive relationship with people runs through the Old and New Testaments. In the Old Testament, when people bowed down to idols and worshiped the gods of the pagan nations, God disciplined them and called them home to himself. In the New Testament, Jesus is lifted up as the only Savior and the unique way to a relationship with the Father.

The idea that people are lost without Jesus is also not a new idea. Some people today dislike the term *lost* and reject the idea that people need Jesus. Some years ago I was training a group of church leaders in evangelism. I used the term *lost* to refer to people who do not have a faith relationship with God through Jesus Christ. Thirty minutes into the training, a woman spoke up with real intensity in her voice: "I don't like that term!"

I honestly had no idea what she was talking about, so I asked her to explain.

She clarified, "I don't like the term *lost*."

When I asked why, she said she felt uncomfortable thinking of people this way. I assured her that the idea made me uncomfortable too, and then I went on to explain that a number of my close friends and family members are still lost (and yes, I used that word). After opening my Bible to Luke 15, I reminded the group that Jesus taught about a *lost* sheep, a *lost* coin, and a *lost* son. I also read them Jesus' life mission statement: "For the Son of Man came to seek and to save what was *lost*" (Luke 19:10). I let the whole group know that God wants us to understand that people without Jesus truly are lost.

This does not mean we should use this term when interacting with people who have yet to cross the line of faith. I have never met a spiritual seeker and said, "Hi, I'm Kevin and you're lost." However, it's entirely appropriate and even necessary for us to see people as lost without Jesus. If this idea or term makes us uncomfortable, so be it. Our greatest need is not to find acceptable terms but to get our hearts to beat with the heart of Jesus. And the clear teaching of Scripture is that Jesus' heart pounds for *lost* people.

When we really understand this biblical truth, we will be compelled to look for lost sheep who are wandering far from God. We will be moved to look past outward appearances and realize that every man, woman, and child on the face of this earth needs what only Jesus can offer. Until they are found by the Savior, they are lost.

Salvation Is Found in Jesus Alone

The Bible teaches with staggering clarity that salvation can be found in Jesus, and *only* in him. This truth has been accepted and taught by Christians throughout the centuries. The Bible teaches us that faith in the one true God alone will save. Yet contrary to the teaching of the Bible, more and more people today are claiming to be followers of Jesus while embracing other religions as valid expressions of saving faith.

Some teachers and scholars have even tried to reinterpret passages in the Bible and redefine their meaning. Ignoring the time-tested insights of great scholars of the past two thousand years, some are seeking to put a new spin on the teaching of the Bible.

Ajith Fernando, a leader of the church in Sri Lanka, regularly battles against this trend to embrace other ways to God. In his insightful and thorough book *Sharing the Truth in Love*, Ajith has a brilliant chapter on the uniqueness of Christ. In the conclusion to this chapter, he writes, "He is unique in an absolute sense. Pluralists say there is no such thing as absolute truth. We cannot say that, for the Creator of the world has given humanity a unique and once-for-all message in the person and work of the Lord of the Universe: Jesus Christ."[9] No matter what the rest of the world might say, as followers of Jesus, we can confidently believe and proclaim that salvation is found in his name (Acts 16:30–31; 2:21; Rom. 10:13).

One example of this effort to reconstrue two thousand years of doctrine and biblical belief is found in contemporary interpretations of John 14:6, in which Jesus says, "I am the way and the truth and the life. No one comes to the Father except through me." This verse has always been held up as a clear teaching, from the lips of Jesus himself, that he is the only way to heaven and that the Christian faith contains the message of salvation found in Jesus alone.

But some authors and speakers today are putting a new spin on the words of Jesus. One prominent teacher writes, "Jesus was not making claims about one religion being better than all other religions. That completely misses the point, the depth and the truth. Rather, he was telling those who were following him that his way is the way to the depth of reality."[10] What these writers emphasize is that Jesus offers the best life possible. They focus on the call to live the "Jesus way" in this world.

I have no problem with the idea that Jesus offers us the best life possible. But that's not what John 14:6 is really saying. If we study the context of the verse, we will find that Jesus is having a conversation with his followers. They are talking about heaven, the gift of eternal life, and the hope of glory. Jesus is pointing his disciples to himself as the unique means of knowing God: "No one comes to the Father except through me." To minimize this biblical truth and teach that Jesus is not making any unique claim about himself or the truth of the Christian faith is at the very least irresponsible. At worst, it is dangerous to the cause of evangelism.

Biblical Christians embrace what the Bible teaches, even when it stretches our thinking or makes us comfortable. If we feel free to modify or redefine clear biblical teaching on topics that we don't like, then all biblical teaching is up for grabs. The truth is that we can't fully understand the wisdom of God. We are limited in our ability to comprehend truth. But the call on our lives is to embrace the truth of the Bible even when our minds can't get all the way around it. I don't have to "get it," but if God's truth "gets me," I will be moved to share the life-changing good news of Jesus.

The Reality of Heaven and Hell

Yet another biblical teaching that impacts our passion for and commitment to outreach is the reality of heaven and hell. C. S. Lewis once wrote, "You have never met a mere mortal." Every person we meet will live forever. The question for each of us is whether we will dwell in the presence of a loving God who paid the price for our sins and invited us to come to him through the amazing grace of Jesus—or spend eternity separated from God in hell.

No one likes the idea of hell. But can we toss aside what the Bible teaches about hell simply because it makes us uncomfortable? For those who believe the Bible is God's Word, that's simply not an option. Declaring that hell does not exist or taking an agnostic posture on this doctrine does not make the reality of hell any less certain. Because we live with a profound confidence that the doors of heaven have been opened for all who embrace Jesus by faith, the reality of hell fills us with zeal and a fresh energy to love, serve, and share the message of Jesus. God has provided *good news* that gives us real hope, despite the awful reality of hell.

In recent years two streams of thought have crept into the church and affected people's understanding of the doctrines of heaven and hell. On the one hand, some people are focused so much on this life and on making the world a better place that they have all but done away with the hope of heaven. A growing number of pastors and writers are teaching the idea that thinking about heaven, preparing for heaven, or being motivated by the hope of heaven creates apathy toward the needs we face in our world today. They would affirm the old adage, "Christians have become so heavenly minded that they are no earthly good."

When we hope for a heavenly city whose foundations were built not by human hands but by God (Heb. 11:10), we should get a clearer focus on what we are called to do in our cities and towns today. Jesus taught us to pray each day, "Your kingdom come, your will be done on earth as it is in heaven" (Matt. 6:10). With a biblically informed perspective on heaven, we can live with a healthy balance of confidence and hope while engaging fervently in the work of serving in this world. The anticipation of heaven's glory does not snuff out a desire to see the kingdom of God break into human history. On the contrary, it gives us an expanded vision of what is yet to come, and it feeds our desire to sacrifice, serve, and unleash the power of heaven in daily life. When we cling to heaven as our hope, we can echo the words of the apostle Paul, even during tough and challenging times: "I consider that our present sufferings are not worth comparing with the glory that will be revealed in us" (Rom. 8:18). With the hope of glory in our hearts, we are empowered to sacrifice our time and finances, take risks, and lay down our lives for the sake of the lost. Living with a hunger for heaven does not stifle our passion to serve in this world—it strengthens it.

On the other end of the continuum, we find those who have no problem with the idea of heaven but are very uncomfortable with the biblical teaching on hell. They try to dance around what the Bible says, and in some cases they simply ignore it. One approach they take is to undermine the Scriptures by saying that the Bible doesn't speak with clarity on this topic. Rather than engage in humble discussion about the teaching of Scripture on this challenging topic, they avoid the Bible by substituting their own opinions, weakening the authority of the very book that speaks words of life and hope.

In *Why We're Not Emergent*, Kevin DeYoung and Ted Kluck write, "The avoidance of hell is not just a 'liberal' problem. Evangelicals in recent decades have soft-peddled the doctrine as well, opting instead for a therapeutic God who encourages our self-esteem. Likewise, some missiologists argue that the missionary enterprise should no longer be seen as a venture to save people from hell, but only as an effort to bring God's kingdom of justice and shalom to all people."[11] The doctrine that people are lost without Jesus is certainly not the only doctrine of the Christian faith. But it is an essential teaching of Jesus. Jesus taught that hell is real and that real people will spend eternity there. Just because we don't like the idea or declare it "barbaric" or see it as "unloving" does not make it any less true.

It is not our prerogative to "do away" with a biblical teaching because it makes us uneasy or our minds can't fully grasp it. As we prepare the soil of our hearts for the work of outreach, we must confidently and joyfully take hold of the teachings of the Bible. Floyd Schneider, in *The Complete Evangelism Handbook*, writes, "The Holy Spirit wields the Scriptures like a knight uses a sword. The sword slices through the thoughts and intents of the heart, revealing to the unbeliever his problem of sin deep within the soul. It wakes him up to the fact that he is spiritually dead to God."[12] Accepting the truth of God's Word has empowered Christians to press forward with the gospel for two thousand years. We too can trust that the Word of God will instruct us in this generation with as much impact as it has for centuries past.

If we believe there is a real heaven and a real hell, we should be moved to evangelize and to reach out in the name of Jesus. If we love people, our hearts should propel us. I heard one of the most convincing arguments for this from an atheist. His name is Penn, the well-known illusionist in the duo Penn and Teller. On his video blog, *Penn Says*, he tells about a man who came to him after a show and gave him a Bible and tried to proselytize him. Here is a portion of his response to that encounter:

> He said, "I'm a businessman. I'm sane; I'm not crazy." And he looked me right in the eye and did all this. And it was really wonderful. I believe he knew that I was an atheist.
>
> But he was not defensive and he looked me right in the eyes and he was truly complimentary. It did not seem like empty flattery. He was really kind, and nice, and sane, and looked me in the eyes and talked to me. Then he gave me this Bible.
>
> I've always said I don't respect people who don't proselytize. I don't respect that at all. If you believe that there's a heaven and a hell, and people could be going to hell or not getting eternal life, and you think that it's not really worth telling them this because it would make it socially awkward—and atheists who think people shouldn't proselytize and who say just leave me alone and keep your religion to yourself—*how much do you have to hate somebody to not proselytize? How much do you have to hate somebody to believe everlasting life is possible and not tell them that?*
>
> I mean, if I believed, beyond the shadow of a doubt, that a truck was coming at you, and you didn't believe that truck was bearing down on you, there is a certain point where I tackle you. And this is more important than that.[13]

If a self-confessed atheist understands that believing in heaven and hell should move Christians to evangelize, how much more should we?

PREPARING THE SOIL

Organic Activity: I Can Do That!

- *Watching Jesus*. Take time in the coming days to learn about how Jesus interacted with lost people. Note his attitude, love, patience, words, and actions in the gospel of John. In particular, see the accounts of Nicodemus (chap. 3), the Samaritan woman (chap. 4), the man by the pool (chap. 5), the woman caught in adultery (chap. 8), the man born blind (chap. 9), and Pilate (chap. 18). You might want to keep a journal with a collection of your insights.

- *Morning Prayer*. For the next week, before you open your eyes each morning, say this prayer:

  Jesus, let my eyes see lost people as you do. Give me vision that pierces through the facades and masks so I can see the depth of people's lostness. As my eyes see, allow my heart to feel what you feel as you look at a world filled with people who are desperately in need of your love and grace.

Personal Reflection

- How can I live with a deeper awareness of the goodness and blessings of heaven that await all who come to the Father through faith in Jesus Christ?

- How can I grow in my awareness that real people will spend eternity separated from God in hell if they refuse to accept the free gift of forgiveness that is found in Jesus Christ alone?

- When non-Christians get to know me, are they confident that I really believe what I say I believe about my faith? What can I do to articulate my faith with greater confidence?

Group Reflection

- Where are you seeing Christians compromise their faith or question core beliefs that have been held by the church throughout its history? Why do you think it is becoming more popular and acceptable to challenge biblical teachings? What are some of the possible problems and consequences of this trend to "question everything"?
- What has helped you to love and grow in your knowledge of the Bible? How can your group members inspire and encourage each other to grow in their commitment to know and follow the truth revealed in the Bible?

Prayer Direction

God of wisdom, your ways are beyond my comprehension. I will never fully grasp all you are and the mystery of your truth. Grant me humility to embrace what your Word teaches even when your revelation spills beyond the boundaries of my understanding. Grant me confidence in your Word and the truth you have revealed through the teachings of the Bible. In this world of confusion and uncertainty, let your truth capture my heart and overflow freely to others. Amen.

CHAPTER 4

The One-Degree RULE

We all have an evangelistic temperature. It can be hot, cold, or somewhere in the middle. It is our responsibility to steward this passion and seek to keep our hearts burning hot and our lives engaged in reaching out.

Jesus went through all the towns and villages, teaching in their synagogues, preaching the good news of the kingdom and healing every disease and sickness. When he saw the crowds, he had compassion on them, because they were harassed and helpless, like sheep without a shepherd. Then he said to his disciples, "The harvest is plentiful but the workers are few. Ask the Lord of the harvest, therefore, to send out workers into his harvest field."

—Matthew 9:35–38

As he approached Jerusalem and saw the city, he wept over it.
—Luke 19:41

When mature believers have a proper understanding of their spiritual inheritance, they cannot stop this knowledge from spilling over into other people's lives. One of the most effective ways to be an evangelist is to manage your life in such a way as to stay mindful of your inheritance in Christ. Stay ever aware of the character of God. Never forget the magnitude of the transformation that has taken strangers and converted them into sons and daughters of God.

—Bill Hybels,
Reaching Out[14]

I was hurrying through Chicago O'Hare Airport on a trip to the West Coast. I landed in one terminal and was rushing to get to a gate that seemed about ten miles away. My first flight was running late, and I wasn't sure I would make it to my connecting gate before they closed the door of the plane. As I blazed across the airport, I found myself weaving in and out of people like they were some kind of obstacle course. When I came up on the heels of an older couple moving way too slow for my liking, I got frustrated and blasted around them. I wasn't seeing people whom God loved. I didn't notice souls who mattered to their Creator. All I saw were barriers to my destination.

Then something divine, mysterious, and glorious happened. God opened my eyes.[15]

In the flash of a moment, I looked at the people coming toward me and saw them in a new way. It was as if God was allowing me to see with his eyes, right inside to their deepest needs and struggles. I saw loneliness, fear, and brokenness walking around wrapped in human skin. I almost wept as I kept moving toward my gate.

I could almost feel people's pain, guilt, sorrow, and grief. In some cases, as I looked into their faces, they seemed just fine. But then I saw past their stoic faces and into their souls. This drove me to pray. I cried out for God to reach down and touch the people around me. They were nameless to me, but I became aware that God knows each one intimately—and loves them.

In that moment my outreach temperature went through the roof! I wanted these people to know Jesus. I knew that God, and only God, could meet the deepest desires of their broken hearts.

By the time I reached the plane, my heart was in a whole new place. It was as if God had graciously stirred the cooling embers and fanned the flames. The fire was back. I hadn't even asked God to raise my evangelistic temperature. It was a gift. By his Holy Spirit he opened my eyes, touched my heart, and set me aflame. For a few brief moments I felt that I was able to see people as God sees them.

Since that day I have sought to pray for eyes to see what God sees and a heart to feel what he feels. Though I don't often experience the same unveiled intensity I did that day in O'Hare Airport, I am learning to see the world around me from a different perspective.

The One-Degree Rule

"Jesus went through all the towns and villages, teaching in their synagogues, preaching the good news of the kingdom and healing every disease and sickness. When he saw the crowds, he had compassion on them, because they were harassed and helpless, like sheep without a shepherd. Then he said to his disciples, 'The harvest is plentiful but the workers are few. Ask the Lord of the harvest, therefore, to send out workers into his harvest field'" (Matt. 9:35–38).

In this passage we are pressed to face a sobering reality. Very often, the problem in the evangelistic equation is not with the world and those who are spiritually disconnected. The problem is with those who are already in God's family. Jesus wants us to see that the harvest is plentiful (many people are hungry for God). It is the *workers* who are not reaping the harvest. Our hearts have become cold. We don't share, care, and pray as we should. In response, Jesus invites us to pray ... for ourselves.

Will you enter in? Will you pray, "Lord, increase my burden for lost people, break my heart for those who don't know you, and increase my evangelistic temperature"?

Every follower of Jesus has an outreach temperature. It can be hot, cold, or somewhere in the middle. This temperature impacts the way we live and interact with those who are far from God. It is our responsibility to steward this temperature and seek to raise it so our hearts burn hotter for those who are lost.

The One-Degree Rule acknowledges the reality that we need to increase our outreach temperature consistently. Over the past few years, I've trained thousands of pastors, leaders, and ordinary Christians to use this simple tool for self-evaluation and motivation.

From One to Ten

The One-Degree Rule involves identifying your personal evangelistic temperature. Using a scale of one to ten, we can identify the level of our evangelistic passion. A ten represents a heart and life that are sizzling hot for reaching out to those who are lost. We pray often, we notice people who are disconnected, we make time in our schedules to be with those who are far from God (and we enjoy it), our lights are shining, we speak of our faith to unbelievers, we share stories of what God is doing in our lives, and we share the gospel (the message of Jesus) in natural ways.

A one represents a heart that is cold when it comes to outreach. We don't pray for lost people, we've become too busy to make space for people who are outside of God's family, we walk past opportunities to let the light of Jesus shine and we hardly notice it, we rarely tell others about our faith and are apprehensive about communicating the gospel of Jesus.

Only you can know your temperature. Only you can name it and identify when you need to take action that will raise your out-reach temperature by one degree. But if you become attentive to this aspect of your spiritual life and are intentional about raising your outreach temperature, you will see it go up consistently. The result will be more regular and more passionate outreach to those who are far from God.

| 1 | 2 | 3 | 4 | 5 | 6 | 7 | 8 | 9 | 10 |

Ice Cold   Sizzling Hot

Take a moment to identify where you are on this scale. Think back over the past month and answer this question: "What is my evangelistic temperature at this time in my life?" Think deeply. Be humble. Say it out loud: "Right now my outreach temperature is a ____."

The biggest issue is not whether you are at three, five, or eight, but that you can identify where you are. I have done this exercise, face-to-face, with many believers, and each of them could identify their temperature.

"I'm at two—I need to heat things up!"

"I'm at a six-point-five, but I would like my temperature to be higher."

The point of this discipline of self-examination is not to get discouraged if our temperature is low or to become proud if it is high. The goal of using the One-Degree Rule is to honestly assess where you are and then ask the next question: "How can I raise my evangelistic temperature by one degree *today*?" If I am at a three, I can take steps to raise my personal temperature to a four. If I am at a seven, I can fan the flames until I am an eight. As my temperature goes up, my effectiveness in outreach increases.

Over the past few years, as I have introduced this simple concept to many followers of Christ, the feedback I have received has been wonderful. One man told me, "I have been seeking to raise my evangelistic temperature by one degree each day, and the results have been amazing. I think about outreach almost every single day. Before I started using the One-Degree Rule, I could go weeks or months and not think about the people in my life who are far from God. Now I pray, share my faith, and love in new ways on a daily basis."

God wants our hearts to burn hot for evangelism. Outreach should flow naturally. The truth is that most Christians do not have the spiritual gift of evangelism, but we are called to be salt and light (Matt. 5:13–16), to be Jesus' witnesses (Acts 1:7–8), and to "make disciples of all nations" (Matt. 28:19–20). Every man, woman, and child who has surrendered their heart to Christ is called to engage in God's plan to reach the world with his grace. We can take time each day to identify our evangelistic temperature and seek to raise it by one degree. This simple process helps to orient our lives toward evangelism.

It is helpful to remember that the point of this self-evaluation is not to compare ourselves with others. Instead, it's about creating an organic lifestyle in which we are always focused on growing in our passion for evangelism. As I've asked various people, "What's your outreach temperature right now?" I've discovered that some people work with a range from about three to six. If they feel their temperature is cooling off, they rate themselves at a two or three. If they are active and passionate about the gospel, they tend to rate at a six or seven. Some people tend to grade themselves harder and would never think to rate their temperature at a nine or ten.

Still others will adopt a higher scale. They might give themselves a six if they are feeling cool in their evangelistic passion and give themselves a nine if they are really tuned in to the Spirit and reaching out consistently. Their personalities and temperaments are such that they use a higher scale. But that's not a problem! Remember, the issue is not so much the specific number you give yourself; it's the effort you make to raise your temperature by one degree. Regardless of how you rate yourself, if you consistently apply the One-Degree Rule, you'll find that outreach will become an organic part of your daily life.

Raising Your Spiritual Temperature

Once you have done an honest and humble self-assessment, the next step is to do something to raise your temperature by one degree. A moment ago you identified your evangelistic temperature. No matter what number you may have said, your goal is the same—take it up one degree! But how do you do it? What can you do to raise your temperature today? As I've worked with church members and leaders over the past few years, we have identified a number of things that can have an immediate and dramatic impact on our outreach temperature.

One of the best ways to stoke the fire and raise our spiritual temperature for outreach is to *engage in prayer consistently*. Consider setting aside a few minutes each day to pray for people God has placed in your life who are spiritually disconnected. Make a list, post a note card, or put a memo in your PDA that reminds you to pray for God to draw these people to himself. Ask the Holy Spirit to speak to them, soften their hearts, and draw them to Jesus. Cry out for God to do whatever needs to be done that they might see their need for a Savior.

Pray that your heart will go out to these people. Jesus taught his followers to cry out to God to send workers for the harvest because the fields are ripe and ready. Let God know you are ready to extend his love and hope. Ask the Spirit to open your eyes to notice people in need. Pray for boldness to serve others in the name of Jesus. And pray for wisdom to know the right time to share your testimony and the message of Jesus.

If you have children, begin asking them about their friends who don't know Jesus. Pray with them for the salvation of their friends.

Ask God to make your home a lighthouse in your community. You will be amazed at how passionately and naturally your children will join in this ministry of prayer. As you pray together, God will ignite your heart and raise your temperature. He will also set in motion a process in which your children embark on the joyous journey of outreach and learn to be stewards of their evangelistic temperature.

Pray for the Holy Spirit of God to give you eyes to see beyond the realm of the physical. Ask God to pull back the veil and let you see and experience people as he does. This prayer will undoubtedly turn your life upside down. Just as Elisha prayed for his servant's eyes to be opened (2 Kings 6:17), we can pray, "Open my eyes so I can see." When God, in the power of the Spirit, opens our eyes to this world as he does, our evangelistic temperatures will rise and ice-cold hearts will melt with a love for those who are spiritually disconnected.

Along with praying for the lost and praying for yourself as you seek to reach out, *make time to be with those who are far from God.* Look at your schedule and honestly evaluate how much time you spend with non-Christians each week. Be sure you don't get sucked into the black hole of church-related activities; instead, push yourself out into your community.

Far too many Christians have become insulated from the world. But Jesus consistently spent time with people who were irreligious and even hostile to the faith. From what we can tell, Jesus even *enjoyed* being around these people, in their homes, at their parties, and involved in their lives. When we spend time face-to-face and heart-to-heart with those who are far from God, our evangelistic temperature is guaranteed to skyrocket! Following in the footsteps of Jesus, we begin to have hearts like his, filled with love and longing for people to know the grace that he offers them. If you have become too busy with church activities and hanging out with Christian friends, it might be time to make some changes in your schedule. Make time for family members, friends, and neighbors who are far from God.

Another way to raise your temperature is to *tell stories.* When you spend time with other Christians, use that time to do some mutual heart igniting. Tell stories about spiritual conversations you are having, about people you know who have come to faith in Christ, and about the steps forward people have taken in their spiritual journey. Talk openly about people you are praying for and reaching out to. Ask other believers what they are doing to share their faith. Talking like this should be an ordinary and organic part of our conversations with other Christians. As we talk together about how God is working among those we are reaching out to, temperatures rise.

Yet another way to boost your temperature is to *make celebration natural*. In your home, church, workplace—anywhere God takes you—make time to celebrate whenever someone takes a step forward in faith. When my brother Jason moved from being a resistant agnostic to a curious seeker, I was overjoyed! I celebrated this with my wife, sons, and some friends who had been praying for Jason for many years. He had not yet surrendered his heart and life to Jesus, but he was becoming more and more open to Christ. He was willing to talk, read books, and investigate the faith. This breakthrough was huge! As we celebrated this step forward in Jason's life, a number of us found our temperatures rising.

When someone crosses the line of faith and receives God's grace through Jesus Christ, temperatures jump! It's like pouring gas on a campfire. The angels of heaven rejoice, and so should we (Luke 15:10). When we hear of a person accepting Jesus, we should tell their story to every believer we meet. This is not a time for quiet and introspective reflection. It's a time to dance, sing, jump, and rejoice!

As we celebrate God's amazing grace and rejoice that another sheep has been found, we'll find ourselves longing for more, and our hearts will cry out to God with renewed passion.

"Spirit of God, my granddaughter is wandering far from you. It breaks my heart and I know your heart aches for her. Please reveal your truth and love to her. Bring her home to you."

"Dear Jesus, my neighbor is so confused, lonely, and broken. Please use me to communicate the hope you can offer him."

"Oh God, pour out your Spirit and touch my mom. She needs what only you can give her."

Stories of conversion remind us that God has the power to soften the hardest of hearts. They propel us forward with renewed energy to pray, love, and share the gospel.

In chapter 3 we looked at the importance of biblical truth. One area we focused on was the reality of heaven and hell. One way to raise our spiritual temperature is to *spend time reflecting on eternity* and on the eternal consequences facing those who don't know Jesus Christ.

The reality of heaven kindles the flame of our evangelistic fire because we long for people to know the glory and wonder of being in fellowship with the God who loves them in this life and for eternity. What an amazing motivator! Through faith in Jesus and by embracing the grace he offers, we can be assured of intimacy with God. We can be restored to communion with our Creator for all of eternity. And while some might worry that the hope of heaven makes us into a bunch of "pie in the sky, by and by" nuts, this clear teaching of Scripture is a powerful motivator. There is a real heaven, it will be glorious, and it will be our home through faith in Jesus.

The hope of heaven has motivated me to share my faith with my siblings and my parents. I have a deep and heartfelt desire for each of them to spend eternity with God. I want to see my family members in heaven. This matters to me more than words can express. I don't pretend that I have the whole heaven thing figured out, but I am confident it will be glorious beyond description and more wonderful than we can imagine or dream. I long for those I love to experience God's love, not just today but in fellowship with him forever in glory.

Reflecting on the other side of the coin can be helpful too. Hell is real, and those who are not saved by God's grace through Jesus Christ will spend eternity separated from God. I wish there were not such a place, but I don't have the right to take out scissors and remove things in the Bible that I don't like. Living with a sober awareness of hell stirs us to help people meet Jesus and make heaven their eternal destination rather than hell.

The existence of heaven and hell is not the only reason we share the gospel, but it is a powerful motivator. When we accept the truth of the Bible, the reality of heaven and hell stirs us to reach out to others with the grace and message of Jesus.

Passion and vision leak. But God is ready to fill us with his Spirit and give us a renewed desire to share his grace and love. By being aware of our own heart condition and outreach temperature, we are well on our way to living lives of organic outreach.

Even if I'm fired up about evangelism today, there's a good chance I'll be apathetic about it next week. Because the forces of hell come against the work of outreach, we'll no doubt become distracted, discouraged, and disillusioned. To counter the tendency to lose our outreach passion, the One-Degree Rule can be a helpful tool. Followers of Christ are wise to do a regular self-assessment of their evangelistic temperature and take steps to increase it by one degree—each day of their lives.

PREPARING THE SOIL

Organic Activity: I Can Do That!

- *Open Your Eyes.* Ask God to open your eyes to see the spiritual reality around you. You might want to read 2 Kings 6 and reflect on Elisha's prayer for God to open his servant's eyes. Ask the Holy Spirit to give you moments when you see behind the veil of the physical world and perceive things with heavenly insight.
- *Check Your Schedule.* Sit down for about fifteen minutes with your calendar or PDA in hand. Look back over the past few weeks and see where you have made time to connect in meaningful ways with people who are not Christians. Note whether you have been making appropriate time to connect with people who are lost. Then look forward a few weeks and see if you can make some more time just to be with people who need to know the love and grace of Jesus.
- *Raise Your Temperature.* Identify your outreach temperature (on a scale of one to ten) and take at least one practical step to raise it by one degree this week. Just watch what happens!

Personal Reflection

- What is my evangelistic temperature in this season of my life?
- What can I do to raise my outreach temperature by one degree?
- How can I adjust my schedule next week to make more time to connect with people who are far from God?

Group Reflection

- How much time do you spend in a normal week with people who are not yet followers of Jesus? What can you do to increase this amount of time?
- What steps can you take to make sure that the light of Jesus shines through when you are with people who are far from God?
- Think of two or three people God has placed in your life who are spiritually disconnected. How can others pray for you as you grow a relationship with these individuals?

Prayer Direction

God of eternity, open my eyes to see the world and people through your eternal perspective. I can be blind to the needs, hurts, and struggles of those I meet. But you see through all the facades. You see people as lost sheep in need of a Shepherd. Help me to see people with your eyes, and teach me to feel with your heart. Raise my evangelistic temperature until it blazes with the same passion that sent Jesus to this world and the cross. For your glory, amen.

CHAPTER 5

Everyone Plays

Evangelism is not a spectator sport. We are all called
to get into the game. God invites every follower of
Jesus to get off the sidelines and onto the field.

"You are the salt of the earth. But if the salt loses its saltiness, how can it be made salty again? It is no longer good for anything, except to be thrown out and trampled by men.

"You are the light of the world. A city on a hill cannot be hidden. Neither do people light a lamp and put it under a bowl. Instead they put it on its stand, and it gives light to everyone in the house. In the same way, let your light shine before men, that they may see your good deeds and praise your Father in heaven."

—Matthew 5:13–16

Follow my example, as I follow the example of Christ.

—1 Corinthians 11:1

The Church of Jesus Christ is growing throughout the world at an unprecedented rate. This is due in large measure to the fact that an ever-increasing number of lay people are realizing their responsibility and privilege of being witnesses to Jesus Christ.

—D. James Kennedy,
Evangelism Explosion

The apostle Paul became all things to all men so that by every conceivable means he could win some. God grant that we will do the same! Begin by being a friend, one who builds bridges and not barriers. In the process, camp close to needs and pray that God will allow you to be part of the solution.

—Joe Aldrich,
Lifestyle Evangelism

I sat in the local township meeting room as people began to congregate. Smiles and nods were passed back and forth as others entered. Some immediately jumped into animated conversations with friends in the room. I was new to the community and was there to learn about serving as a coach in the local AYSO (American Youth Soccer Organization).

Being the father of three young boys, I had signed up to coach for two reasons. First, I wanted to spend time with my boys and enjoy the great game of soccer. Second, as a new pastor in the community, I wanted to build relationships and meet some folks who were not part of the church. My involvement in AYSO was a great combination of family and outreach, and I eventually coached more than twenty teams over a decade of working with this program.

As the AYSO leader began to explain the philosophy of this soccer program, I was uncomfortable ... at first. I had coached high school soccer a few years earlier, and to be honest, I have a bit of a competitive streak. But one of the philosophies of AYSO is that everyone plays regardless of skill or ability! They believe that when everyone plays, all the kids win. What really matters is not the final score.

The leader went on to explain that at the younger ages most of the kids don't even know the score or care who wins. As I listened, I was a bit skeptical about the idea that winning is not about getting more goals but about just playing the game. I listened and tried to get in the AYSO spirit. I raised my hand and asked, "Is it okay if we tell the kids which direction to kick the ball and that they should actually try to get it into the goal?" He caught my attempt at humor and said, "Of course!" Then I asked, "What if the kids inquire as to why they should kick the ball into the goal? Can I tell them the team gets a point?"

This question led to a great conversation about the importance of getting all the kids playing, the value of keeping score, and how to teach kids to win and lose well. It became clear that the program was not against competing, keeping score, or acknowledging that there are winning and losing teams at the end of the game. The *greater* value was simply to engage all the kids in the sport of soccer.

At one point in the local soccer program, some coaches had wanted so badly to win that they were playing only certain kids while others sat on the bench. Sadly, for several of the kids who had signed up to play, soccer had become nothing more than a spectator sport. Some of the kids were being set up to lose before the first game was even played. The AYSO experience was designed to change that philosophy by getting all the kids running, playing, and learning.

Over the next decade I adopted the AYSO philosophy and was amazed by what I saw. Rather than leaving some kids on the bench and playing them only when we "had to," we decided to give everyone the *same* amount of field time. Kids blossomed! Skills grew! Some of the boys and girls I coached amazed me. There were a number of kids who, when they first came to practice, looked like they would not play well. But when they learned that they would be getting field time, that the team would be depending on them, and that they were needed, these kids rose to the task.

Other team members caught the vision as well. They began to call greatness out of kids who easily could have spent the season sitting on the bench. One boy I coached for a number of years became a great goalie. He was focused and always encouraged the defenders he played with; he even started scouting for other goalies he could mentor and cheer on. The vision was spreading to the kids—they were getting it.

Lessons from AYSO

Everyone plays and everyone wins. The AYSO philosophy is just as true when we think about Christians and outreach. I have discovered a number of parallels with my experience as a youth soccer coach and how we do evangelism in the local church.

In the church, when everyone plays, we develop a healthy sense of team. On my AYSO teams, there was no animosity or competition between the players; we knew we were in this thing together. Each player stepped up and did his or her part. As Christians, we can learn from this model. When followers of Jesus commit to get in the game and do their part in reaching out to the lost, a sense of partnership develops. We begin to cheer each other on. It's not about a few players out there running, sweating, and giving 100 percent while others sit by and watch. When we *all* heed the call to evangelism, we *all* experience the joy of being part of a team striving for the greatest goal in the entire world.

While coaching youth soccer, I found that many of the kids had amazing skills that had never been called out of them. If they had been allowed to stay on the bench, they never would have discovered these abilities. And when those kids started playing and contributing, smiles showed up on their faces—there was joy! The same is true when we all commit to engage in evangelism. People who may have said, "I can't do that," soon discover that God can use them to share his grace and his message of hope. Smiles break out and joy overflows. As people accept the challenge, get onto the field, and engage in outreach, they sense the filling of the Holy Spirit and see their gifts being used. They experience the joy of watching lives changed by God's power.

I learned one final lesson while coaching AYSO. Some kids really thought they would be happier sitting on the sidelines instead of playing in the game. On almost every team were a kid or two who were there because their dad or mom thought they should, "Get off their behind, stop playing so many video games, get outside, and do something active." Often parents would tell me they had enrolled their son or daughter in the soccer program for this very reason. But I could also tell from the look of concern written all over the child's face the first time I talked about running or juggling a soccer ball. They were nervous about getting involved on the team. But in almost every case, by the end of each season, these kids were some of the most enthusiastic players on the team.

I have seen the same reality unfold as I have watched people enter into the glorious calling of evangelism. Some people are willing to get involved in outreach only because they sense that their heavenly Father wants them to get off their spiritual rear ends and do something active. They are driven by a sense of duty but lack any real enthusiasm. To their surprise, as they engage, as they pray for lost people and reach out to their neighbors and friends ... wow! The very people who were content to sit on the bench and cheer others on become fired up with a passion for souls ignited by God's Holy Spirit. Outreach becomes something they grow to love, something that feels natural for them—it becomes organic.

In God's plan for outreach, everyone plays. There are no spectators or bench warmers when it comes to evangelism. God wants everyone on the field, even those who feel like they can't do it or have nothing to contribute. God wants you to get involved. The world needs you to get in the game.

You Are God's Plan

In the early 1980s I read a powerful book called *Lifestyle Evangelism* by Joe Aldrich. It is still one of the best books written on relational evangelism, and I recommend it highly.[16] Aldrich writes a fictional account of Jesus and his return to glory after his life on this earth:

> Even in heaven Jesus bore the marks of His earthly pilgrimage with its cruel cross and shameful death. The angel Gabriel approached Him and said, "Master, you must have suffered terribly while down there."
>
> "I did," He said.
>
> "And," continued Gabriel, "do they know all about how you loved them and what you did for them?"
>
> "Oh, no," said Jesus, "not yet. Right now only a handful of people in Palestine know."
>
> Gabriel was perplexed. "Then, what have you done," he asked, "to let everyone know about your love for them?"
>
> Jesus said, "I've asked Peter, James, John, and a few more friends to tell other people about Me. Those who are told will in turn tell still other people about Me, and My story will be spread to the farthest reaches of the globe. Ultimately, all people will have heard about My life and what I have done."
>
> Gabriel frowned and looked rather skeptical.... "Yes, but what if Peter and James and John grow weary? What if the people who come after them forget? What if way down in the twenty-first century, people just don't tell others about you? Haven't you made any other plans?"

And Jesus answered, "I haven't made any other plans. I'm counting on them."[17]

What a sobering thought. We are God's primary plan for spreading the message and the good news of his Son! As the Holy Spirit leads, fills, and empowers us, we become his messengers.

Be Salt: I Can Do That!

Jesus said, "You are the salt of the earth." But what was he really getting at? Though this image points to many spiritual realities, we need to identify with at least two of these when it comes to outreach.

SALT MAKES PEOPLE THIRSTY

There is a good reason Mexican restaurants give free chips to patrons waiting to order their dinners. It's the same reason restaurants and bars give out free popcorn, pretzels, or nuts. And we all know why. Salt makes us thirsty! In restaurants and bars these snacks are a simple vehicle to deliver salt to the customer's mouth. As customers get thirsty, they buy lots of drinks. People who eat salt develop a longing for something to quench this thirst.

As followers of Christ, we know that Jesus is the Living Water (John 4:4–15). Only he can quench our spiritual thirst and refresh our souls. The woman Jesus encounters in John 4 is drawing water from a well to quench her thirst. But her thirst is more in her soul than in her mouth. She has spent years dropping a bucket down the well every day, but she has never been satisfied. She has also thrown the bucket of her heart down well after well, seeking satisfaction from man after man, but she is still empty inside. When she meets Jesus, she discovers a man who can quench her inner thirst—her spiritual longing. She excitedly runs into town and tells all the people she has been avoiding about this man, Jesus. Her transformed life becomes like salt to their souls. They begin to thirst and wonder. "Could this be the Messiah? Is he the one who can refresh our lives and quench the longing of our arid hearts?"

God wants you and me to be salt in this world. Our passion for God, a life of integrity, an overflowing joy, a sense of peace, and an authenticity in our relationships should cause others to thirst for what we have. Our satisfied and refreshed spirits can be like salt that causes others to say, "I want that kind of love, joy, peace, patience, gentleness ..." When we live and work in close proximity with people who are far from God, our lives of faith should naturally point them to the well that offers them true living water.

SALT PRESERVES

In the ancient world, people used salt to preserve food and keep it from spoiling. Even today, most canned goods are laced with sodium. It keeps the food fresh. Salt is a powerful preservative.

God wants us to be agents of preservation sprinkled throughout the world. When the lost see the power of God in our lives, we are preserving a witness to God's continued presence and involvement in this world. And people inevitably are drawn to Jesus.

The preserving impact of authentic Christians can be manifested in many ways. In a world where immorality reigns almost unchecked, our commitment to purity and holiness becomes a preserving factor in society. But this commitment isn't a matter of judging and condemning every person and action that is ungodly. If judgment was our goal, we could spend all of our time pointing out what is wrong in this world.

Instead, our commitment to holiness means that we seek to model conduct and attitudes that reflect God's heart. When a Christian business owner runs his company with integrity and honesty, he has a preserving influence and reveals the presence of God. Each time a high school student who loves Jesus refuses to cheat on a test, resists giving in to sexual temptation, or seeks to care for another student who has been marginalized, she becomes a preserving factor on her campus. Every time Christians speak with honesty, care for the environment, protect the oppressed, pay their taxes, stand for the value of human life, resist racism, love their neighbor, or do anything that helps build a stronger and healthier world, they become preserving factors and God receives glory. Over time, others begin to ask us why we are different, why we care so much, and why we live such a countercultural existence. In those moments we can point to the one who saved us, who empowers us to live as beacons of hope and holiness.

If you are a follower of Christ, you are called to be salt in this world. Your life will cause people to thirst for the living water of Jesus. Your attitudes and actions will have a preserving impact, and people will see God at work in your life. So let your life be salty! Throughout the rest of this book, you will discover many ways to do this.

Be Light: I Can Do That!

Jesus said, "You are the light of the world." Once again, our Savior uses a common picture to inspire his followers to be agents of spiritual influence right where he has placed them. The image of light prompts many different thoughts. Here are just two to consider.

LIGHT ALLOWS US TO WALK CONFIDENTLY

Have you ever experienced utter darkness? It can be paralyzing. My wife, Sherry, and I discovered this early in our marriage when a storm caused a large branch to fall on the wires that brought electricity to our apartment. Our area suffered so much damage that we were told the electricity wouldn't be restored for several days. We decided to make the best of it and use lots of candles. It would be fun and romantic—or so we thought.

Late one night I woke up and had to use the bathroom. I could not find the matches, and I hadn't thought to leave a flashlight by the bed. It was pitch black. I could not see my hand in front of my face. But nature called—so I made my way to the bathroom. Very slowly. I knew there was nothing on the floor to trip me up, but I still shuffled my feet cautiously. I knew there was nothing hanging from the ceiling, but for some reason I kept waving my hands in front of my face to make sure the way was clear as I inched forward. The whole production took much longer than it would have if I could have just flipped on the light.

In our world, people are shuffling and stumbling as they try to walk forward in life. They are living in darkness, and God is the light they need. Jesus came as heavenly light to a dark world. The light that shines from us is *reflected* light, a reflection of Jesus' light. When people look at us, they should see a confident trust in the Savior, a boldness rooted in our faith in him. This confidence is not an arrogant posture that says we know it all and have everything in life figured out. Rather, it is a humble certainty that God is on the throne, that we are walking in his light, and that we don't have to live like those who stumble in the darkness. As unbelievers see this attitude in our lives, they will be drawn to the light of God that shines through us—Jesus Christ.

LIGHT DRIVES AWAY FEAR

In a fear-filled world where anxiety runs rampant, Christians can show what it means to live life free from fear. In my teenage years, my dad and I did a lot of backpacking and camping in the mountains of California. As the sun set and darkness fell, we always appreciated a roaring fire. Not only did it provide warmth and chase away unwanted bugs and wild animals, but the fire pushed back the fear of darkness. The light of a blazing fire brought comfort.

Our culture is infested with fear. Economic times are uncertain, wars are being waged around the world, terrorism is on the rise, gangs run wild in many cities, global climate change is a hot topic, natural disasters occur around the globe, and countless other fear-producing topics are covered in minute detail on the daily news and on the internet every time we power up our computers.

More and more people in our world today are being gripped by anxiety, worry, and, in some cases, raw terror. But when a follower of Jesus walks in the light and shines as the light, the fears of this world flee. The apostle Paul writes, "Do not be anxious about anything, but in everything, by prayer and petition, with thanksgiving, present your requests to God. And the peace of God, which transcends all understanding, will guard your hearts and your minds in Christ Jesus" (Phil. 4:6–7). As we spend time around spiritual seekers and they see a peace and fearless attitude through our faith, the light of God becomes visible to them. Our humble confidence in the power and goodness of God becomes a witness to a dark world trapped in fear.

Jesus does *not* say to us, "If you would like to be light in this world, sign up to take a class at your church called 'Lighting Up My World' and give it a try." Instead, Jesus declares to all who bear his name, "You *are* the light of the world." It's time to let our lights shine so people will see the good things of God and give him glory.

Finding Your Unique Way of Doing Outreach

Many people run from the idea of outreach because they feel it requires them to be abrasive and confrontational. But there are as many ways to do evangelism as there are different kinds of people. Your unique way of doing outreach grows organically out of who you are. The key is to invite the Spirit of God to direct you as you look for approaches that match your wiring and personality.

For many years I watched Grandma Lois do her outreach ministry. Lois had the gift of greeting people with a loving and gracious spirit, both at church and in her neighborhood. Every Sunday, Grandma Lois (everyone knew her as "Grandma") moved around the church lobby like a heat-seeking missile. She loved to hug the kids in the church and always stopped to bless those who had been there for many years. But her primary mission was greeting and embracing new people. She kept her eyes open for visitors and people who were new to the church. She had the heart of Jesus and was eager to offer God's love to those who were visiting.

When Grandma Lois spotted people she'd never met, she immediately headed straight for them. If she was chatting with church members, she politely excused herself and made her way toward the visitors. Even though she wasn't very fast, you could tell when she had someone in her sights. Her arms reached out toward them as she'd move in for a hug! There was just no stopping her. For some reason, when Grandma Lois came at people with her arms outstretched, no one ran away. She learned visitors' names and a little bit of their family history and often answered a few questions about the church, leaving them with a parting blessing. Then she headed over to her husband, Peter. You see, Peter and Lois were an outreach *team*. They worked together. Each one of them had their own strengths. Lois would do the greeting, hugging, and gathering of important information. Peter was the keeper of names and data.

Grandma Lois offered a warm heart, but unfortunately, her memory wasn't nearly as sharp as Peter's. So year after year, she did the greeting and Peter stored the information. A few weeks later, when a family returned to visit the church again, Lois first headed to her husband and said, "Peter, remind me about that family." He gave her names and details—everything Lois had told him. Then she headed over to greet the family again, confident she had the right information.

What a team!

Each of them was engaged in reaching out in a way that fit their personality and utilized their gifts. If Peter had tried to greet people with a big hug, they might not have been quite as receptive. Hugging was for Lois! But if Lois had been responsible for remembering all of the information, she would have felt overwhelmed. As a team they were simply amazing.

This beautiful partnership continued for many years until Peter fell ill. After a prolonged battle, Pete passed away. Grandma Lois came to me one day after his passing and said, "Pastor Kevin, I don't know if I can do my greeting ministry anymore." I was shocked! I knew she loved to meet and bless people, and I knew she was sad about Peter's passing, but I could not understand why she felt like her outreach ministry should end. I asked her to share what was on her heart. That was when I first learned about their partnership. Grandma Lois told me how Peter had been her memory and data keeper all these years. "I am afraid I will meet someone one week and then the next time I see them, I might not remember their name. I don't want them to feel bad if I forget their name. Peter was always here to help me with the details. I wonder if I should keep greeting people."

My heart broke for her. But it would have broken even more if she had stopped her outreach to the new people in the community. We had a great conversation that day, and Grandma Lois concluded that it would be okay if it took two or three meetings with people before she remembered all their names. She promised to keep reaching out, even though her partner of so many years wasn't there to share in the ministry.

As I write this book, nearly a decade has passed since Grandma Lois lost her husband, best friend, and partner in outreach, but she is still finding visitors and greeting them with a hug and the love of Jesus. If you happen to visit Corinth Reformed Church in Byron Center, Michigan, you just might find a beautiful elderly woman coming at you with her arms outstretched. If she locks on you, don't run. Resistance is futile! Grandma Lois won't stop until you have been hugged, greeted, and blessed in the gracious name of Jesus.

Peter and Lois VanHaitsma are a great picture of how we each have our own way of doing outreach. The key to successful outreach is discovering ways that fit us and that unleash the natural evangelistic potential God has placed in us.

My wife, Sherry, does most of her outreach from a place of serving people in times of need or listening to people's hurts and struggles. She has the gift of compassion, and people are drawn to her. She doesn't go marching around saying, "I have to find someone to reach out to." The truth is that Sherry does *not* have the spiritual gift of evangelism. She simply lives, loves, cares, and serves people. As she does what comes naturally to her, friendships are forged, the love of God is shared, and the good news of Jesus touches lives.

My outreach style is very different from Sherry's. Evangelism is one of my strongest gifts. I don't have the gift of compassion like my wife does. But I find that I can naturally enter into spiritual conversations with almost anyone. I don't really have to work at it. In a restaurant, at the counter of a store, in an airport, with friends and family—conversations about God's love, presence, and amazing power just come up. That's my style.

As you think about your own opportunities for outreach and pray for your evangelistic temperature to rise, you'll discover that you have a unique style. In parts 2 and 3 of this book, you'll find some practical ideas to help you bring content to your style, but the approach you use needs to be birthed out of who you are. Your life history, passions, personality, sense of humor, and communication style all help to shape the way you do outreach.

Some years ago, evangelistic leaders Bill Hybels and Mark Mittelberg wrote a book called *Becoming a Contagious Christian*.[18] In recent years, this book and the related training curriculum have been updated and revised. The *Contagious Christian* materials help Christians identify various styles of sharing the faith. The genius of this approach is that it recognizes that there are many different biblical models of doing outreach. Some people are naturally *confrontational*, and this style works well for them as they reach out. Some take an *intellectual* approach, while others lean toward *interpersonal* outreach. People whose natural evangelism style is *testimonial* tell stories of God's grace and power that draw people to the Savior. Some Christians are naturally *invitational* and connect spiritual seekers to people and places where God's presence is evident. Many people, like my wife, *serve* faithfully, and through their Spirit-anointed acts, people become open to the message of God's love. The key point is that we all have a unique style of reaching out.

You might not have the gift of evangelism, but you *are* called to engage in the ministry of outreach. You are popcorn on the table of this world—be salty! You are a flashlight in the cellar of this world—shine! You have a natural way of doing evangelism, so take time to discover your style and let Jesus' presence enter into each of your relationships. As you continue into the next part of this book, you'll learn ways to scatter the seed of the gospel and pour out God's living water to help the seed grow. Now that the soil of your heart is prepared, it's time to think about the next step in organic outreach.

PREPARING THE SOIL

Organic Activity: I Can Do That!

- *Be Salty.* Are you living an attractive Christian life? Being a Christian doesn't mean you pretend that everything is perfect and Christians never struggle. It means you authentically express the goodness of living for Jesus. Take time to list at least ten reasons you are thankful to be a child of God through faith in Jesus. Meditate on these reasons and be open to ways you can share them with someone who is not a Christian. Honestly tell others how much you love being a child of God; tell them about the peace he brings, the strength he offers in hard times, and the hope you feel in moments of challenge. As you share why you love being God's child, pray that those who hear your stories and watch your life will begin thirsting for what refreshes your soul—the living water of Jesus.

- *Shine Light.* In this world of confusion, you have experienced God illuminating your path many times and in many different ways. As you encounter people who are struggling with a lack of direction or a sense of confusion about their future, consider sharing the wisdom you have received that brings light to your path. It might be a passage from the Bible, an insight you received in prayer, or counsel from a wise Christian brother or sister. As you seek to shed God's light on other people's situations, be sure to let them know where you got this wisdom.

Personal Reflection

- Am I convinced that God is calling me to engage in outreach in new and fresh ways? If not, what is standing in the way? If so, what's my next step?
- Who is one Christian I have watched over the years who has modeled being salt and light in this world? What can I learn from this person's example?
- What kind of outreach activity that I've engaged in has felt the most natural? What has felt the most forced and foreign to me?

Group Reflection

- Why do some people tend to sit on the bench when it comes to outreach, and what can be done to help them get on the field and engage in this important calling?
- As a group, what are some activities you can do and actions you can take that could have a preserving impact on your community?
- As you look at each other, what do you see in each person's history, temperament, and personality that could be used by God for organic outreach?

Prayer Direction

God of light, you shine in the darkness. You bring direction and drive out fear. Let your light shine in and through me. For too long I have resisted your call to engage in outreach. Now I'm beginning to understand. I am starting to see and believe that you really can use me to share your love and good news in this world. Help me get off the sidelines and participate in your life-changing, light-bringing ministry in this world. Amen.

PART 2

Planting and Watering

God invites us into his mission of reaching the world with the grace of Jesus. We get to help prepare the soil of our lives, of the world, and of the hearts of those who are far from God. Along with this, we have the privilege of scattering the seed of the gospel and watering that seed. The apostle Paul writes, "What, after all, is Apollos? And what is Paul? Only servants, through whom you came to believe — as the Lord has assigned to each his task. I planted the seed, Apollos watered it, but God made it grow" (1 Cor. 3:5–6). This passage is a powerful reminder that only God can change a life, but he still invites us to be involved in his world-transforming activity. We can *plant* and we can *water*.

Joe Aldrich puts it this way: "The Christian's primary calling is to witness, to be a light, to play the music. His strategy is low pressure, long range. He is a seed planter who knows when to plant the seeds. He thoroughly trusts God to bring the harvest. This does not mean he is lazy. It simply means he knows you have to plant seed, cultivate it, water it, and wait for the harvest."[19] In this section, we will investigate some of the different ways that we can be part of God's amazing work of scattering and watering the seed of the gospel.

The Naked Truth about Evangelism

Most of us have heard the story of *The Emperor's New Clothes*. It's a memorable tale with a powerful message. The emperor was arrogant and wanted the finest clothes in the land — he deserved them! He hired the top fashion experts and they got to work on his new wardrobe.

But there was a problem. The fashion experts turned out to be scoundrels. They knew more about deceit and thievery than about clothes and fashion. So they worked and worked and worked. Finally, when the emperor's patience was beginning to wear out, they allowed him to see the fine clothes that were still being fashioned. They assured the arrogant monarch that only those who were truly wise and noble could see and appreciate the materials used to make his new clothes.

When the emperor looked at the cloth on the loom, he saw nothing. When the charlatan tailors held up the "clothes," there was nothing but air. Everyone else declared how beautiful and elegant the clothes were. Even the emperor's counselors agreed that the clothes were exceptional. They didn't want to look unwise or foolish, so they just played along with everyone else.

Too embarrassed to admit that he could not see the clothes, the emperor agreed that the clothes indeed were the most beautiful he had ever seen. This process of deceit continued until the emperor's new wardrobe was complete. In short order the money was in the pockets of the "tailors," and the emperor was marching down Main Street with great pomp and circumstance ... and nothing else!

Finally, someone blew the whistle. A little boy watching the parade exclaimed, "The emperor has no clothes!" At that moment, when the truth was spoken out loud, everyone knew what was happening. The veil was suddenly lifted. The kingdomwide denial and deceit were quickly replaced with clarity and truth. The emperor was buck naked!

This story reflects a painful reality when it comes to contemporary evangelism. A lie has been sold to Christians throughout the world. It has been repeated over and over again by people who seem to know what they are talking about, to the point that the subjects of the kingdom are fearful to admit that "the emperor has no clothes." I believe most of us are aware of the lie. We know that what we are hearing about evangelism is wrong. But who are we to disagree with conventional wisdom? Who are we to blow the whistle and say, "This is a lie"? Who are we to declare that the emperor is naked?

So what is this deceitful message that is being paraded all over the Western church? What is the lie so many followers of Jesus are hearing and accepting?

It's the idea that Christians are too forceful with their faith and need to back off, settle down, and be more subtle.

Over and over in the past decade we have heard it from speakers and read it in articles: we Christians are scaring people off with our bold and pushy evangelistic tactics. Our words are too direct, and we are offending the world and driving people away from Jesus! Since our blunt and blatant strategies are counterproductive, our best course of action is to just calm down. The only way we will reach this generation is by backing off.

It's time for someone to stand up and declare, "This is a lie."

I don't believe, in most cases, that the caution against "overzealous" evangelism is malicious, but it's beginning to have a profound impact on followers of Jesus. People read articles and hear seminar speakers talk about all the damage being done by overzealous Christians. Or maybe they watch a video portraying a sidewalk evangelist going up to people with a bullhorn and screaming religious slogans—scaring and offending people and driving them away from faith.[20] Believers hear these messages and think, "That's right—we should not be like the bullhorn guy. We should back off and quiet down. The last thing we ever want to do is offend anyone."

Truth be told, the bullhorn guy is a myth, a caricature that doesn't really exist. Don't get me wrong; I realize a few people out there have tried to bludgeon people with the gospel, and it's likely there is a small percentage of Christians who end up scaring people away with loud and invasive tactics. But is that really what most followers of Christ are like? Does the average Christian need a warning to back off from their overzealous commitment to evangelism? Do you?

An Honest Picture

As I travel and speak around the United States, I've been conducting an informal survey of church leaders. I've asked more than a thousand of them this simple question: "Is the problem with the people in your church that they are overzealous and too forceful in bringing the gospel to their friends, neighbors, and community?" After listening to the answers, I then ask, "How many of you feel that what your church members need is a warning to back off and be a little tamer when it comes to sharing Jesus with others?" Take a wild guess how many of these leaders raised their hands and affirmed that the people in their Christian communities need to dial back the intensity of their outreach?

The answer—none. Not a single person!

Then I ask these same church leaders, "How many of you would say the greater need is for the people in your congregation to be more impassioned, more committed, and more zealous about sharing their faith?" Though it's not a scientific study, the best count I have to date is about one thousand out of one thousand people. In other words, I haven't encountered a single leader who has complained that the people in their congregation are pushing too hard in the area of outreach. Keep in mind that these were leaders from across the country, from various denominational backgrounds, and from every walk of life. And the gatherings where I asked for input on these important questions were not evangelism events. They were leadership training seminars and small group ministry events.

What is my point? The emperor has no clothes! We have believed the lie for too long, and the results have been tragic. Many followers of Jesus have refrained from going out in the world scattering seeds and watering because they are afraid of *offending* people. Church leaders are becoming too fearful and embarrassed to call the believers in their congregations to step out and do the work of evangelism.

Two thousand years ago Jesus said, "The harvest is plentiful and the workers are few." This is just as true today as it was then. People in the world are hungry for spiritual truth. The problem is not with the world; it is with the church. We have far too many believers who are not willing to become workers in God's harvest fields.

We must stop telling believers to back off and settle down. Let's not kid ourselves: for every "bullhorn Christian" scaring people away, there are a couple of thousand believers refusing to scatter and water the seed of the gospel in Jesus' name.

It's time for us to agree with Jesus and speak the truth when it comes to reaching out in love with the message of God's grace. It's time for the church to rise up and for followers of Christ to enter into the harvest. The next time you hear someone say that Christians need to be subtler in the work of evangelism, you can politely tell them, "The emperor has no clothes!"

CHAPTER 6

The Unseen WORK

Praying *for* People

Prayer is the cornerstone of all effective outreach. We unleash heavenly power when we pray for lost people. We are also called to pray for ourselves and other believers to enter the harvest fields with God's good news.

When they arrived, they went upstairs to the room where they were staying. Those present were Peter, John, James and Andrew; Philip and Thomas, Bartholomew and Matthew; James son of Alphaeus and Simon the Zealot, and Judas son of James. They all joined together constantly in prayer, along with the women and Mary the mother of Jesus, and with his brothers.

—Acts 1:13–14

"Ask the Lord of the harvest, therefore, to send out workers into his harvest field."

—Matthew 9:38

For our struggle is not against flesh and blood, but against the rulers, against the authorities, against the powers of this dark world and against the spiritual forces of evil in the heavenly realms. Therefore put on the full armor of God, so that when the day of evil comes, you may be able to stand your ground, and after you have done everything, to stand.

—Ephesians 6:12–13

The condition of the church may be very accurately gauged by its prayer meetings. So is the prayer meeting a grace-ometer, and from it we may judge the amount of divine working among people. If God be near a church, it must pray. And if he be not there, one of the first tokens of his absence will be a slothfulness in prayer.

—Charles Haddon
Spurgeon

When I met Jason, I liked him immediately. He was bright, warm, and very funny—a dangerous combination. After I was asked to come to his church and help raise the evangelistic temperature for the leadership and the whole congregation, we met for lunch and talked about evangelism. Jason is a full-time staff member and leader at Faith Reformed Church in Dyer, Indiana and serves as a multisite pastor on the Valparaiso campus.[21] This dynamic congregation has a simple, memorable, and powerful mission statement: "Reaching the disconnected, growing the connected."

The lead pastor, Bob Bouwer, had asked me to coach the key leaders in the church in the area of "reaching the disconnected."

I explained to Jason that my role was to help him develop a clear evangelistic vision for his areas of ministry in the church. He seemed excited. He knew this was part of the commitment of the church leadership team and was interested in learning ways to move his ministry out of the church and into the community. He wanted to see the church reach the spiritually disconnected. I could sense Jason's anticipation about how we might partner in helping members of Faith Church reach out with the gospel.

Then I spoke a line that I have used hundreds of times over the years in developing, mentoring, and coaching leaders. I said, "Jason, you can't lead what you don't live." I explained that his first step in outreach leadership would not be to train volunteers, develop new programs, or form a special committee on evangelism. Instead, it would be to examine his own life and make sure he was living an outreach-oriented lifestyle. I talked about how he needed to raise his own outreach temperature and make sure he was connecting with the lost people God had placed in his life.

Jason's response was honest and typical. He said he absolutely believed in evangelism and even told me he had taken a class on evangelism in seminary. He said that while he was in the class, he seemed to have all kinds of opportunities to connect with spiritual seekers and share God's love and message. But when the class was over, his focus on outreach cooled off.

Jason wanted me to know that he was strongly in support of evangelism, but right now, making time to hang out with spiritually disconnected people was not really an option for him. He was invested in raising his young family, building a Christ-honoring marriage, taking seminary classes, participating in a special ministry training program, and working full-time at the church.

Jason believed in the call to evangelism. He was sold out on the concept. He wanted his ministry to be highly evangelistic. The real problem was that he thought he was too busy to engage in it personally. He thought there was no room in his life for being with friends and neighbors who were spiritually disconnected.

Jason was overwhelmed by a busy schedule and felt that it would be difficult to engage in meaningful relationships with spiritually disconnected people. Instead of saying, "You have to make time," I took a circuitous route to get where I wanted our conversation to go. I was a bit sneaky. I didn't ask Jason to spend more time with his neighbors. I didn't challenge him to adjust his schedule. I didn't even ask him to focus on adding some new outreach-oriented aspects to his ministry.

Instead, I asked Jason a simple question.

"Do you have time to pray?"

What do you say to a question like that? How can we say no?

Of course Jason agreed to pray. He committed to ask God to open his schedule, to create opportunities for his life to be salt and light. We prayed together and asked the Holy Spirit to move in Jason's life and schedule. He later told me that the very same afternoon he was prompted to pray even more. He came before God and opened his heart and life to do outreach. He didn't feel he could make the time or space, but if God kicked a door open for him, he would walk through it.

Sometimes asking a person to pray may seem simple and benign. The truth is, nothing we do as Christians is more dangerous than prayer.

That very evening there was a knock at Jason's door. A neighbor stood outside—and he wanted to talk. During the ensuing conversation, the neighbor asked Jason if he would be willing to teach him about God, and they agreed to begin a Bible study together. After some time, the neighbor asked if he could invite others to this informal gathering. This regular time together led to some wonderful connections and deeper relationships right on the street where Jason lives.

Only a few hours after Jason prayed about it, God had opened doors!

When Jason told me about what happened, I wasn't surprised. I asked him, "Now do you have time for your spiritually disconnected neighbors?" He smiled and said, "Yes!"

Praying for People

When God's people pray, heaven shakes, strongholds are broken, and power is unleashed. More is accomplished through prayer than through all of our slick outreach brochures, multiple-step programs, and big evangelistic events combined. Don't get me wrong, though. I believe in using great print pieces, outreach training programs, and large outreach events. But without prayer, these activities are empty of power.

As a young believer I was able to participate in a Billy Graham Crusade held at the Big A in Anaheim, California. What struck me most about this mass outreach event were the countless hours of prayer offered by thousands of people before Billy ever came to town. Billy Graham often said that if the believers in a community were not united in prayer, he wouldn't commit to come do a crusade. Over the days of this event, thousands of people came to faith in Jesus Christ. The prayers of God's people were the groundwork for this unleashing of Holy Spirit power.

There are all sorts of ways to pray for people who are spiritually disconnected. The issue is not finding "the right way to pray" but discovering creative ways for you to pray each day. One approach to prayer might feel natural for a time, and then another approach might lead you to effective prayer during another season of life. Allow yourself to be creative and flexible, but always make sure that you are spending time praying regularly for revival and for people to experience the life-changing grace of Jesus Christ.

PRAYER WALKING

One way to pray for God's movement in the lives of people is to identify an area or territory you will commit to cover in prayer. It might be a school campus, a street, an office building, a restaurant, or some other location. Prayer walking is the practice of moving consistently through an area and praying as the Holy Spirit leads.

If you decide to prayer walk (or prayer drive) your street or neighborhood, commit to do so at least weekly. Begin walking (or driving) and quietly lift up prayers for God to move and break out in each life and home. Don't pray out loud, but pray quietly in your spirit. If you are walking with another person, you can pray out loud and casual onlookers will think the two of you are having a conversation. Here are some specific guidelines to help direct your prayers:

- Pray for families and individuals you know. Pray for them by name and ask God to meet needs and touch lives.
- Ask the Holy Spirit to open eyes and soften hearts. God is moving in every home, but people often miss his activity. Pray that people will notice the presence and work of God.
- Pray for believers in your community to let the light of Jesus shine in and through them. Ask for gentle boldness as Christians give testimony to their faith.
- Pray for broken families to be healed, shattered hearts to be restored, loneliness to be lifted, and needs to be met in the power of Jesus.
- Ask the Spirit to bring a conviction of sin that creates a longing for the cleansing that only Jesus can offer.

As you prayer walk, listen for the voice of the Holy Spirit. You might not know exactly how to pray, but if you listen, the Spirit will direct you. For instance, you might feel directed to pray for freedom from fear as you pass a house, but you don't even know the people who live there. Respond to the Spirit's leading and pray for people in that home to be set free from the bondage of fear.

There's something wonderful about having a specific territory you decide to cover in prayer. It could be a mall or an office complex. Whatever the location, make a point of being there regularly to intercede. You will be amazed at how God grows your heart for the people who live, work, or study in this place. You will also have the joy of watching God do great things in the very territory where you have committed to pray.

When I began serving a church some years ago, I felt led to pray over a specific community to the south of the church's gathering place. Early on in my prayers for this community, I found myself crying out for freedom from sexual sin and bondage. I thought this seemed like a strange way to pray since I had no reason to think this community had spiritual strongholds in this area. But the Spirit kept prompting me to pray and intercede for families with sexual brokenness, so I did. The people and families I met from this area, both church attenders and community members, seemed healthy and happy. Still, I continued to pray as the Spirit led.

Almost a year later, through my pastoral ministry I began to hear stories about the unusually high level of addiction to pornography, sexual brokenness, and abuse in this community. There had been a cycle of sexual sin in this town for decades, but it was buried deep and no one talked about it.

It was heartbreaking to learn of the shattered hearts and lives hidden in many of those homes. But I was reassured of God's presence and power when I realized that he knew the needs of this community and had directed me to intercede in ways that I could not have known on my own. In the coming years many people who had faced fear and brokenness due to sexual sin were set free and experienced God's healing touch. I am confident I was given divine insight into the needs of this community because I spent time praying in a focused area.

TRIPLE-FIVE PRAYERS

I have heard many versions of what I am about to suggest, so I give credit to all those who have used a similar prayer approach. Another way to enter into evangelistic prayer is simply by lifting up five people for five minutes, five days a week. This approach gives you one minute to pray for each person. Make a list of people you care about who are far from God. Keep the list in your Bible, tape it to a mirror in your home, store it in your PDA, or put it some other place where you will be reminded to pray on a regular basis.

If you are not sure how to pray, here are five simple suggestions:

1. Pray for their hearts to be soft to the presence and promptings of God.
2. Ask the Holy Spirit to convict them of sin and help them see their need for God's grace.
3. Pray for God's blessings to flow into their lives and for them to recognize his goodness.
4. Ask God to break down and remove the obstacles in their lives that keep them from seeing and responding to the Holy Spirit's presence.
5. Surrender your life, time, and words to God. Ask him to use you to reflect his grace, serve faithfully, and share his good news when the time is right.

PRAYERS FOR WORKERS

Jesus called us to pray for the Lord of the harvest to send workers into the harvest fields. Spend time crying out to God for a fresh work of the Holy Spirit in the lives of those who call themselves followers of Jesus. Pray for new boldness. Pray for Christians to be committed to connect in the world and not to allow themselves to be cloistered in a church subculture.

You might even want to identify a handful of Christian friends who don't seem very engaged with lost people. Make a list and commit to cry out for the Spirit to stir their hearts to love people who are far from God. Fulfill Jesus' command by praying for hundreds, thousands, and millions of believers to be ignited to share their faith in organic ways, right where God has planted them.

God of the harvest, send us out. Open our eyes to see that the fields are white for harvest. Remind us each day that the work is yours, but you invite us to be part of what you are doing in this world. Give us gentle sensitivity and passionate boldness. Help us to speak with clarity, to love with intensity, and to model the presence of Jesus in the world. Send us out,

Lord. Ignite our hearts and let your light shine through us in your name. Amen.

SCRIPTURE PRAYERS

Through the centuries, Christians have allowed the Word of God to shape their prayers. By reading a Bible passage, meditating on it, and even committing it to memory, you will be amazed at how your prayers can be elevated and empowered. When we pray Scripture, our prayers are always on target. Here are some passages you might use as a launching pad to evangelistic prayer:

- Matthew 9:35–38
- Ephesians 2:1–10
- Philippians 1
- Colossians 1
- 1 John 5:1–12

You can use one of two simple ways to get started in praying Scripture. One is simply to read a verse or section and let the words become your own, directed to God. The second approach is to let the words of the Bible launch you into prayer as you read a verse or two and then personalize the message, letting the theme drive you deep into prayer for a certain person or situation, wherever the Spirit leads. As you pray Scripture, you will be amazed at how God shapes powerful prayers you never would have come up with on your own.

LISTENING PRAYERS

Another way to pray for family and friends is to ask the Holy Spirit to shape your prayers. This approach requires taking time in silent waiting as you ask God to form your prayers. In many cases, the Spirit will whisper and give you an exact prayer for a specific person. As this happens, you can lift up your prayer with confidence because you know God is leading you.

As you come before God in a posture of waiting, place the person before God. For instance, before you wait and listen, you might say:

- Lord, you know my boss can frustrate me at times and demand so much from all of us at work. I often dream of how his life might change if he knew you. I am confident that you love him and want him to open his heart to Jesus. Guide me, Lord, and speak to me. How would you have me pray for my boss?

- O God, you know how I love my mom. I want so much for her to meet Jesus and receive his love, grace, and power in her life. My heart breaks for her, and I know her life would be filled with new meaning and joy if she could meet you face-to-face and embrace Jesus as Savior. How would you have me pray for my mom? Direct me, Lord. Speak to me, Spirit of God.

Once you have expressed your heart, wait quietly and listen. You will want to have a piece of paper and something to write with at your side. As the Spirit speaks, write down the impressions that are on your heart and the way you believe God wants you to pray.

I remember praying for a dear family member some years ago. The clear leading of the Spirit was to pray for God to send "committed and 'regular-looking' Christians" into his life. That might seem like a strange prayer, but this family member sees most Christians as "strange." For the next couple of years, I prayed for God to send some ordinary Christians into his life.

In another situation, as I prayed for a man I know, the Spirit directed me to ask for humility in his heart. He was so self-secure that he thought he didn't need God—or anyone else for that matter. Over the coming months, I prayed for his pride to be broken and for a humble and receptive spirit to grow in his heart.

One of the most surprising prayers I was directed to lift before God is this: "Dear God, strip away the wealth, possessions, and props this couple holds on to so they will see their need for you." I felt strange praying this way, but I knew the Spirit was leading. So without ever telling the couple, I prayed for them to lose their wealth and the security blanket of material goods if that was what it would take for them to receive an inheritance in heaven that will never perish or fade (1 Peter 1:4). Maybe that prayer sounds harsh, but I believe it was a prayer born of love for these people. Moreover, it was how God called me to pray, so I lifted up this request with confidence.

Listening prayers might be new to you. The idea of God directing you in how to pray for a person could feel strange at first. But as the Spirit begins to shape your supplications, you will feel a new power and boldness as you intercede for your friends and family members who are not yet followers of Jesus.

FRUIT OF THE SPIRIT PRAYERS

I am absolutely convinced that God offers the best life possible. Following Jesus does *not* guarantee we will never struggle or face difficult times. But what people want and need most in this life is exactly what God offers us through his Spirit. Think about it. What do people long for?

"I want to feel loved and be near people I can love in return."

"I'm doing all I can to find true happiness and lasting joy, but they just seem to elude me."

"I just want to feel a freedom from anxiety and worry in this troubled world—I want peace!"

Do these desires sound familiar? Where in the world can we find love, joy, peace, and all our hearts long for? The very things people hunger for most are found in lasting abundance in God alone!

Over the past decade I have meditated on the fruit of the Spirit and prayed for this fruit to grow in the lives of those I love. I began doing this for my wife and three sons. I would reflect prayerfully on Galatians 5:22–23: "But the fruit of the Spirit is love, joy, peace, patience, kindness, goodness, faithfulness, gentleness and self-control. Against such things there is no law." And as I thought of each fruit, I identified one that seemed to be needed in the life of each of my family members. Then I committed to pray for this fruit to grow over a number of weeks. This approach has been an amazing experiment in prayer, because I never told my family what I was doing. With time I saw the very fruit I was praying for begin to grow in their lives.

Almost every person who walks this earth longs for love, joy, peace, patience, and all the other fruit of the Spirit. If they see these characteristics growing in the lives of Christians, they will desire what we have. When they inquire how we can be so patient or ask about the source of our love, we can point to the God who lives in us. Every believer should pray for the fruit of the Holy Spirit to grow in their lives. Then we can prepare ourselves to tell others about the source of the kindness, gentleness, and self-control that are blossoming within us.

WARFARE PRAYERS

Scripture assures us that our battle is not against flesh and blood (Eph. 6:12–20). If we are not ready and committed to enter into spiritual warfare, we will not see a great harvest of souls for the kingdom. Every time we seek to do outreach, we are entering into enemy territory. We need to fortify ourselves as we engage in the battle. Satan will not stand by idly as we seek to reach people who are presently under his control and dwelling in his domain.

Several excellent books have been written on the topic of spiritual warfare and are included in the Recommended Resources section in the back of this book. I want to offer three words of counsel as you seek to pray against the work of the devil in this world and in the lives of those who are under his sway.

First, *ask God for discernment to see where the enemy is at work*. Too often we don't notice the movement and tactics of the enemy because we are not tuned in to the reality that our battle is not against flesh and blood. Keith Green, a wonderful songwriter from the 1970s and early '80s, wrote a song from the perspective of the devil called "Satan's Boast." In one verse of the song Satan says, "I used to have to sneak around, but now they just open up their door. No one is watching for my tricks, since no one believes in me anymore." May these words not be true of us. Once we become profoundly aware that the enemy of our souls wants to thwart our outreach efforts and keep people in his grasp today and forever, we can begin praying for eyes to see where the enemy is at work and what tactics he is using.

Second, *pray against the work of the devil in the name of Jesus*. As we resist the devil, he will flee (James 4:7). Moreover, he who is in us is far more powerful than the one who is in this world (1 John 4:4). When we pray in the name of Jesus and in the power of his blood, we pray with heavenly authority. When we stand in the glory of the resurrection of our Savior, sin and death will flee. Stop for a moment to meditate on these words of Scripture:

When the perishable has been clothed with the imperishable, and the mortal with immortality, then the saying that is written will come true: "Death has been swallowed up in victory."

"Where, O death, is your victory?
Where, O death, is your sting?"

The sting of death is sin, and the power of sin is the law. But thanks be to God! He gives us the victory through our Lord Jesus Christ.

Therefore, my dear brothers, stand firm. Let nothing move you. Always give yourselves fully to the work of the Lord, because you know that your labor in the Lord is not in vain.

—1 Corinthians 15:54–58

As we pray in the power and authority of the one who conquered sin, death, and the devil, we will see strongholds fall and the kingdom of God advance.

Third, *commit to pray with other believers*. God has placed us in community with other Christians, and there is strength in numbers. One of the ways we battle the enemy is by praying in partnership with other believers, crying out to God and going deep in prayer with Christian friends and neighbors—even if they go to another church. What a radical idea! We can find a cluster of like-minded believers who have a passion for outreach and understand spiritual warfare and commit to pray for and with each other. If you have Christian friends at your workplace, consider prayer walking together one day a week on your lunch break or after work. You can do the same with other believers who live near you, meeting one day a week to prayer walk together and experience the power of community. The key is realizing that we don't have to travel this road alone and that we are stronger and safer when we learn to pray in community.

Praying for those who are spiritually disconnected is one of the most powerful and active things we can do. It should be the first action we take in any kind of outreach. Use these tools to get you started, but be sure to make them your own. Let praying for lost people flow from a heart that beats with the heart of God, and your prayers will be organic.

PLANTING AND WATERING

Organic Activity: I Can Do That!

- *Try a New Way of Praying.* Go back through the chapter and pick two kinds of prayer you have not tried before (or done recently). Take a week to experiment with this kind of outreach prayer and see if it feels natural for you. Try prayer walking, triple-five prayers, Scripture prayers, listening prayers, fruit of the Spirit prayers, or warfare prayers.

Personal Reflection

- What steps can I take to engage more passionately in praying for those who are not yet in God's family?
- Who do I know who models a life of committed and fervent prayer? What can I learn from this person's example and lifestyle?
- What are some obstacles that keep me from praying, and what can I do to remove them?

Group Reflection

- Tell about the kind of prayer that most naturally ignites your heart as you intercede for family members, neighbors, and friends who are unbelievers.
- How might you encourage and fortify each other as a small group in your commitment to pray for those who are lost?
- Which of the various prayer ideas in this chapter seem most natural for you, and how might you incorporate them into your prayer life?

Prayer Direction

Lord Jesus Christ, you opened the door to the throne room of the Father through your sacrificial death on the cross. When you died, the curtain in the temple was torn in two and full access to the presence of the Father was made possible. Help me approach the throne of grace with boldness and cry out for those who are still far from you. I know you love lost people far more than I do. Teach me to pray, to cry out, to intercede for those who do not yet know there is a God who loves them. Make me powerful in prayer, devoted to lifting up those who are wandering like sheep without a shepherd. In your name, amen!

CHAPTER 7

The Wonder of ENCOUNTER

Praying *with* People

Praying with unbelievers is an opportunity for God to show up and reveal his power. Organic outreach is propelled forward when we learn to pray with those who are not yet part of God's family.

"If my people, who are called by my name, will humble them-
selves and pray and seek my face and turn from their wicked
ways, then will I hear from heaven and will forgive their sin
and will heal their land."

—2 Chronicles 7:14

When he came down from the mountainside, large crowds fol-
lowed him. A man with leprosy came and knelt before him and
said, "Lord, if you are willing, you can make me clean." Jesus
reached out his hand and touched the man. "I am willing," he
said. "Be clean!" Immediately he was cured of his leprosy.

—Matthew 8:1–3

Our greatest need today is a deep, thoroughgoing, Spirit-
wrought, God-sent revival. Such revivals as far as man's agency
is concerned always come in one way—by prayer.

—R. A. Torrey,
The Power of Prayer

Today there is great need of intercessors: first, for the needy
harvest fields of the earth, born of a Christlike compassion for
the thousands without the gospel, then for laborers to be sent
forth by God into the needy fields of earth.

—E. M. Bounds,
Essentials of Prayer[22]

My father was in the hospital awaiting heart surgery. The doctors had told us that he would die without the surgery, and even with it, there was still a possibility that we would lose him. It was a critical time, so I flew from Michigan to California to be with my dad, mom, and siblings. My wife and sons would follow a few days later. We explained to our boys that this might be the last time they would see their grandpa.

Although he is not a Christian, my dad loves his children and respects our faith commitment. His personal beliefs put him somewhere between agnosticism and friendly theism. So when we asked Dad if we could gather around his bed and pray for him before his surgery, he didn't object. All five of his children and a few of our spouses gathered with my dad and mom for a time of intercession. As we prayed, I could sense the presence and power of God. I was filled with hope. We prayed for his heart, both physically and spiritually.

Over the next few days, the surgery went perfectly, Dad recovered rapidly, and the doctors were amazed. They weren't sure whether his heart would grow stronger with time, but it became healthier than it had been in a long time. I am confident that all of this was a direct answer to our prayers.

Though my dad and mom have not yet given God the credit for the healing my dad has experienced, the kids in the family know that God has spared his life and given him more time to live. We hope it will be a fresh chance for him to receive the grace offered freely in Jesus Christ. His physical heart has been healed. We continue to pray for transformation in his spiritual heart.

My parents are not yet Christians, but they are very open to prayer. Over the years, I have prayed for each of them on various occasions — during hospital stays, at special family gatherings, at renewal of their wedding vows on their fiftieth anniversary, and on other occasions when I had the opportunity. These times of prayer have provided an opportunity for the Holy Spirit to enter into our relationship and for God to show his power and presence.

Praying with People

We can engage on a whole new level in our relationships with non-believers when we pray *with* them. It is amazing how open people are to prayer. Even if they don't believe in the Christian faith, many are glad to receive prayer. My dad captured the attitude best during one of the first times I asked if I could pray for him. His response was, "It couldn't hurt!"

Over the past thirty years, I have asked thousands of people if I could pray for them. Not a single person has yet said no, including committed Chrfistians, cultural Christians, agnostics, and even atheists. I'm not saying that everyone will welcome prayer, but in my experience, most people will gratefully receive prayer when it is offered. In particular, when people have shared an area of struggle in their lives, a place of pain, an experience of loss, or even a moment of incredible joy, they are especially open to an offer of prayer.

I've noticed that many followers of Jesus spend a lot of time and energy trying to get people to come to church. But have we ever thought of bringing church to where people already are? When we pray with someone who is not yet a follower of Jesus, they get a chance to experience the presence and power of God. These moments can happen in our cars, at home, in a break room at work, on the sideline of a child's sports event — anywhere we find an opportunity!

The process isn't complicated or difficult. When you are interacting with someone who shares a deep burden or a great joy, simply ask, "Would you mind if I took a brief moment to pray for you?" If they say, "Yes, I would mind; please don't pray for me," then honor their request and don't pray at that time. You can still lift them up in prayer on your own. The truth is, most people will be glad to have you pray.

If you ask for permission to pray with an unbelieving family member or friend and they say yes, pause right then to offer up a simple prayer. Here are seven simple suggestions:

1. *Keep your prayer brief.* In most cases less than a minute is wise.

2. *Use common language.* Don't make your prayer flowery and don't use the King's English. Let your words of prayer be conversational and natural.

3. *Extend a hand if it is appropriate.* If you feel it would be taken the right way, take the person's hand or place your hand on their shoulder. There is power in touch.

4. *Pray for the person's specific need or joy.* Focus your prayer on what they shared with you and don't wander to other topics. Keep it simple; don't turn your prayer into a chance to preach a sermon.

5. *Pray in the name of Jesus.* There is power in Jesus' name. God already knows and cares about the person you are praying for. Make sure they know to whom you are praying and who to thank if the prayer is answered.

6. *Check in to see how things are going.* After a week or two, check in and see if the need has been met or if the joy is continuing to flow. If so, give God the glory. If the need persists, keep praying.

7. *Be sensitive to location and volume.* If you are in a public place, step out of the flow of traffic. You may be comfortable with prayer, but it might be new territory for the person receiving it. Seek a little privacy if possible. Also, pray quietly. Remember, the only people who need to hear are you, the person you are praying for, and God.

I have discovered that people will begin to seek you out and ask for prayer once they realize you are serious about lifting up their needs before God. Even nonbelievers have asked me to pray for them. As God answers prayers, doors are opened for spiritual conversations and the sharing of the gospel.

Pictures of Praying with People

I could tell story after story of different times I have prayed with people who were not believers. Some are serious and others are quite funny. Praying with others can be an organic way of sharing our love for Jesus.

JAIL PRAYER

Once, while doing ministry at a local jail, our team members asked the men what we could pray for. Many at the service were believers, but some were not. Some came to the service simply to get out of their tiny cells for about forty-five minutes. At first, no one responded to the offer of prayer. I asked again, adding, "We're serious—we want to pray for you!"

One of the inmates said, "You won't pray. You'll leave here and forget about us."

I replied, "We do want to pray, and we'll do it right now."

The men's eyes lit up and hands went up all around the holding area. Our team members went to each one, listened to his needs, placed a hand on his shoulder, and prayed. I think every man in that room received prayer. We lifted up parole hearings, prayed for freedom from addictions, cried out for wives and children who were struggling, and asked God to touch and change the lives of these men. When our allotted time was up, we were still praying and the guards had to ask us to close the service. These hardened convicts began with a cynical refusal to share their needs because they thought we were not serious about praying for them. Many ended up hugging our team members with tears in their eyes and thanking us for our prayers.

BLESS ME

Another time I was in a restaurant by myself and had been studying for a sermon. As I stood at the front counter paying the bill, the young woman behind the register saw my Bible. "Oh, are you a pastor?" she asked.

I told her I was.

She blurted out, "Will you bless me?"

I was slightly taken aback but honored to receive the invitation. "Sure," I said.

What happened next was precious. She closed her eyes and leaned as far as she could across the counter. So I extended my hand and placed it on her forehead. Right in the entrance to the restaurant, I prayed:

The LORD bless you
and keep you;
the LORD make his face shine upon you
and be gracious to you;
the LORD turn his face toward you
and give you peace.

—Numbers 6:24–26

She opened her eyes and thanked me. I felt the presence of God's Spirit there with us, and as I walked out, I knew God was at work.

FAMILY PRAYER

In another situation I was conversing with a family member who was hurting over some decisions being made by a person she cared about deeply. I knew she wasn't a Christian because I had shared the gospel in the past and she had rejected it. Even so, after she shared her hurt and concerns, I felt I needed to ask if I could pray for her and the situation she had told me about. Knowing she might be resistant, I took a chance and asked if I could take a moment to pray for her.

She thought for a moment and said, "I would like that very much." She sat next to me on the couch and I took her hand. As I prayed for her and her friend's needs, she squeezed my hand firmly. When I closed the prayer "in Jesus' name" and said amen, she had tears in her eyes. Again, God showed up. She didn't cry out, "What must I do to be saved?" but I'm convinced she felt the presence of the Holy Spirit and saw that prayer is real.

RESTAURANT PRAYERS

I like to ask servers in restaurants if they have any needs I can pray about. I just say, "Hey, when we get our food, we're going to have a short prayer. If you think of anything we can pray about for you, just let us know when the food gets here." It is amazing how many servers come back with a need. If they don't, it's no problem; I don't bring it up again. But many of them share very vulnerable and honest requests. Quite often these people are not Christians, but they do want prayer.

One woman shared that she was trying to quit smoking and was having a hard time. We ended up praying with her over a number of months and celebrated her victory over this addiction when she finally kicked the habit. Another server told us she was pregnant. which was already quite apparent. She asked if we would pray for her unborn child. When the meal came and we were ready to pray, she stood right at the edge of the table and kind of pointed her stomach toward me to get the maximum impact of the prayer. She had a Catholic heritage but wasn't active in practicing her faith, and she was so thankful to have someone pray for her baby. This simple moment led to ongoing prayer for this woman over the coming months whenever we dined at her restaurant. It also led to celebration when her son was born.

One of the more humorous moments came when a server said, "Yes, I would love to have your prayers." She then leaned close to our table and whispered, "I'm looking for a new job. I want out of here!" We prayed for her but were sure to whisper our prayer so that management didn't get word of her impending departure.

I have found that these restaurant prayers can open the door for great conversations, friendship, authentic sharing, and even presentations of the gospel. The prayers aren't manipulative or forced; they're just a natural part of relationship.

Many Christians have never thought to pray with an unbeliever. It seems strange and out of place ... until you do it. The truth is that many of the people you know who are not followers of Jesus would love to have you pray for them. They know you believe in God, and they suspect that you believe there is power in prayer. When you lift up their need or joy, you confirm what they already know about you as a Christian.

When you pray with an unbeliever, all kinds of amazing things can happen. God's presence can be felt as he draws near in the power of the Spirit. God's power can be seen as prayers are answered. Spiritual seekers can see that your faith is real and you have a relationship (a friendship) with God. They see that your faith is not some religious game—it's real! Doors are opened for ongoing spiritual conversations as they ask you questions like, "Do you really think what happened was an answer to prayer?" And you'll find that your heart will begin to connect with others in new ways as faith becomes a part of the fabric of your relationship.

You might find yourself wondering, with all these benefits, why not take a chance and offer to pray with people in your life who are not yet Christ followers? Honestly, I can't think of any reason to wait!

Inviting People to Pray

My brother Jason watched my life as I became a Christian and eventually went into full-time ministry. For a while, he showed some interest in my faith and even attended church for a short time, but he soon pulled away and took the posture of a staunch agnostic. Over two decades I prayed for Jason countless times. I prayed for God to open his heart and eyes to the presence of Jesus. I often thought about what a great Christian Jason would make and what a wonderful impact God could have through his life if he were to receive the free gift of grace offered in Jesus Christ.

Whenever Jason and I were together, I enjoyed being with him. When my family moved two thousand miles away from Orange County, the frequency of our hang-out times was greatly reduced, but when I was in town, we always got together. I wanted so much for Jason to know the powerful love of Jesus, so when we got together, I lived out my faith without apology, sharing stories of God's goodness and talking openly about Jesus. Jason never recoiled or pushed me away. He recognized that my faith was real, but it was my thing, not his.

After I'd spent many years praying and seeking to reflect God's presence and grace to him, Jason began to open his heart. He started asking more questions, reading Christian books, and investigating the claims of Jesus and the teachings of the Christian faith. In the midst of this season of spiritual searching, Jason came to Michigan to visit and spend time with my family. We had a great time together and enjoyed some wonderful conversations about faith.

During his visit I remember encouraging Jason to begin praying. I encouraged him to do what I have encouraged many spiritual seekers to do over the years—talk with God. This might seem strange to some, but I have found that it is actually quite powerful. We believe that God is alive, that he still speaks and moves in our lives. Imagine what could happen if people were to cry out to him and seek his face—even before they received the grace of Jesus. Do you think God will listen? What are the chances that God might respond to those who honestly seek him?

When I encourage nonbelievers to begin praying, I give some simple direction. Here are a few organic prayers that seekers can lift up:

1. *God, I don't know if you are real, but if you are out there, please show yourself to me.* As a spiritually disconnected person asks God to reveal himself, they invite the Holy Spirit to begin moving in their life. God wants to reveal himself, and for spiritual seekers, a prayer of openness is a great start to the process of recognizing the presence of God right where they are.

2. *If you are out there, God, and you love me, will you help me feel your love?* People are longing for love and wanting to know if there is a God who has affection for them. They want to know if God really cares. When an unbeliever invites God to reveal his love, we know this is a prayer that Jesus died to answer. If a person begins praying this way, they will also be more open to hear you share stories of God's love experienced in your daily life as well as the story of God's love poured out on the cross of Calvary.

3. *If you are real and as powerful as people say, could you answer my prayers and meet my needs?* God answers prayer, and not just the prayers of believers. Over the years, I have talked with many spiritual seekers who have started praying for God to help them, and he has answered in clear and powerful ways, leading them to ask, "Is this really the hand of God?" As they have discovered that God is already working on their behalf, they are open to get to know God even better—through his Son, Jesus.

Over the years, I have been amazed at how many people have been open to making time in their lives to pray to God long before they accept Jesus as Savior. As they have prayed, God has spoken, revealed his love, and shown his face. This has led to deeper spiritual conversations, encounters with the Holy Spirit, revelations of God's powerful presence, and presentations of the gospel.

For my brother Jason, entering into focused prayer was just one of many ways he investigated and tested the Christian faith. With time his eyes and heart were opened and he finally surrendered himself to Jesus Christ. One of the most joyful days of my life was when I baptized Jason in the Pacific Ocean, just a few miles from where I had been baptized more than twenty years earlier.

And my suspicions were confirmed! Today Jason is a wonderful Christian man with a godly wife and three beautiful children. He decided to go back to school and complete a master's degree in theology and worship. Even as I write these words, my previously agnostic and resistant brother is praying about the possibility of entering into some kind of full-time Christian service. I am convinced that the prayers of other Christians, and Jason's prayers, before and after he received Christ, have been a powerful part of this transformation.

As followers of Christ, it is incumbent upon us to pray *for* those who are not yet part of God's family. We should also have the courage to ask people if we can pray *with* them. As we do this we stand beside them and invite them into the presence of God by lifting up their needs and joys. In addition, we can help people along on their spiritual journeys by encouraging them to lift up honest, seeking prayers. God will hear. God will answer. And lives will be changed for eternity.

PLANTING AND WATERING

Organic Activity: I Can Do That!

- *Try a Restaurant Prayer.* The next time you go to a restaurant and your server is not too busy, take a moment to say, "I'm going to have a prayer before my meal. If you have a need I can pray for, please feel free to let me know about it when the food gets here." Just see what happens. Worst possible scenario — they just won't be able to think of a need. Best possible scenario — they will share, you will pray, and God will move.

- *Invite Someone to Pray.* If you are connecting with someone who is not a believer but you feel the relationship is in a safe and healthy place, consider encouraging them to begin praying. Suggest one of the three prayer directions in this chapter and challenge your friend to give prayer a try.

Personal Reflection

- Who are two or three non-Christians God has placed in my life? What are some of their needs today? What are their joys? How would they respond if they shared a struggle and I said, "Would you mind if I took a moment to pray with you?"

- What might keep me from asking my unbelieving friends, "May I pray with you?" Are these obstacles enough to keep me from trying?

- What might happen if my non-Christian friends allowed me to pray with them? How might my relationship with them grow if they began to freely share needs and joys with me and I began to consistently lift them up in prayer?

Group Reflection

- If you have had a chance to pray with someone who is not a believer, tell about your experience. How did this time of prayer impact your relationship? What opened the door for prayer?
- If you have never prayed with a nonbeliever, what might keep you from doing so? What might help you become bolder and more willing to try praying with others?
- As you ponder the idea of praying with nonbelieving family members and friends, what thoughts go through your mind?
- What might happen if the spiritually disconnected people in your life started praying to God and asking him to reveal himself, show his love, and answer their prayers?

Prayer Direction

God of heaven and earth, it amazes me that you invite us to enter your presence through the grace of Jesus. I want to learn to pray with my family and friends who are still far from you. I long for them to experience your presence and love. I know they will feel your Spirit as we pray in the name of Jesus. Please give me courage to take a risk. Help me stand side by side with people who do not yet have a relationship with you and pray with them. And when I do, please answer in amazing ways. Amen.

CHAPTER 8

Incarnational
Living

People need to hear about Jesus, but they also need to see him. As his ambassadors on this earth, we are to reflect his love, show his heart, and incarnate his presence wherever God sends us.

Your attitude should be the same as that of Christ Jesus: who, being in very nature God, did not consider equality with God something to be grasped, but made himself nothing, taking the very nature of a servant, being made in human likeness. And being found in appearance as a man, he humbled himself and became obedient to death—even death on a cross!

—Philippians 2:5–8

When we allow God to mark our manner, alter our attitudes, and burnish our behavior, people will naturally ask, "What is it about him? What is it about her?" They'll take note that we have been with Jesus—and have undergone dramatic change. This gives glory to God as we become walking billboards that proclaim his reality and redeeming power.

—Gary Thomas,
The Beautiful Fight

How did Jesus know so much about people? He lived, walked, and talked with them and displayed genuine interest and concern for their welfare. He met people on the streets, on the hillsides, in the fields, at meals, at work in fishing boats, at prayer, at weddings, on the roads. Such observational research energized by the Holy Spirit provided keen insights.

—James Engel and
Wilbert Norton,
*What's Gone Wrong
with the Harvest?*

I walked into the pizza shop and was immediately impressed. The guy behind the counter was tossing pizza dough high into the air and catching it with one hand. Each time the dough spun upward, it would stretch a little more until it fit the pan perfectly. It was fascinating.

My friend leaned toward me and said, "Amazing! How does he do that?"

I muttered back, "I think I could do that."

My wife would tell you that I am a bit of a loud talker. I don't notice it, but apparently I project more than I realize.

This was one of those moments.

The guy behind the counter froze in midtoss and stared at me through a cloud of flour. I gulped as he said, "You think this looks easy?"

I apologized and explained to him that I played freestyle Frisbee and that tossing a pizza looked a lot like spinning a disc. He kept his eyes on me as he slowly wiped his hands on his apron, reached under the counter, and pulled out a Frisbee. "Let's see what you can do."

I was surprised by his request, but I took the Frisbee, spun it on my right pointer finger, passed it under my left leg, tossed it into the air, and caught it behind my back. As I finished my impromptu job interview, he said, "How would you like to make six bucks an hour tossing pizzas?"

That was twice what I was making flipping burgers at Carl's Jr., so I said, "Yes!"

I had no idea God was orchestrating a divine appointment, but a few days later I discovered that making pizzas was not the main reason I got this new job.

Marc was one of the delivery guys at Munchies Pizza. He had a warm personality to go with a big smile and a hearty laugh. He seemed to like everyone at the pizza place—except me. We were both in high school and I thought we would get along great, but after a few days I realized he had something against me; I just didn't know what it was. Marc didn't say much to me when he was in the store, and he spent most of his time on the road delivering pizzas.

I can still remember our first conversation like it happened yesterday. We were standing in the back room folding pizza boxes and stacking them up to the ceiling. I was trying to engage him in conversation, but he would only grunt monosyllabic responses. Eventually I joined him in silent mode as we assembled piles of boxes.

Finally, Marc spoke up. "You get high?"

"Not anymore," I said.

"Get drunk?"

"No."

He looked at me, making eye contact for the first time. I could tell he was very skeptical at this point. He asked his third question in a tone of confused worry: "You get down, don't you?"

Strike three! I explained that I had a girlfriend, but we had decided not to have sex.

The best way I can explain the look on his face is to say that it was one of stunned wonder. I could see the wheels turning as he tried to find a category for this seemingly normal-looking high school guy who didn't smoke weed, get drunk, or have sex with his girlfriend. He muttered a one-word question as he tried to put the pieces together: "Why?"

I responded with a question of my own: "Do you really want to know?" He assured me he did, so I shared about my new faith in Jesus. I told him what my life was like before, how I had grown up in a home with no religious heritage, and how Jesus was transforming my life every day. I talked about my joy and the purpose I had found in being a Christian. He listened with great interest and obvious curiosity. As strange as it might seem, I was able to share my testimony and the story of Jesus during our first conversation.

Marc became a friend that night. He even confessed that he had decided not to like me because I had taken his job. It turns out he was in line for a job tossing pizzas (which paid more than the delivery guys got) and the boss had hired me instead.

I apologized. He accepted my apology. And we pressed on.

I found out that Marc was a party animal of the John Belushi–*Animal House* genre. He had no shame when it came to telling others, including me, about his excesses and conquests. That first conversation led to months of friendship, frank discussions, and many new experiences in my life. Marc knew that I didn't get high, get drunk, or sleep around, but he still invited me, unreservedly, into his life.

I had no idea I was doing "incarnational ministry," "friendship evangelism," or "organic outreach." I just started hanging out with my new friend and tried to let my faith be authentic and visible.

Marc loved parties, so I went with him to a number of them. He was into street skating, so I bought some equipment and we spent hours skating and talking. Marc had a fascination with finances and investment, so we talked about that.

I went to church youth events, so he came along. I loved the beach, so we hung out there. I was passionate about the Bible, so I shared what I was learning. Over the months, our friendship grew and Marc became curious about Jesus and the Christian faith. His party lifestyle stopped looking so attractive. The Christian friends I connected him with had a level of joy, peace, and purpose that fascinated him.

After some time, Marc decided to surrender his life to Jesus and cried out for the forgiveness only Jesus can offer. He was a changed person. Soon after his conversion, Marc began praying for his family and friends to come to faith. He was letting his life become a testimony as he stayed connected with people who were far from God. Within a short time of becoming a follower of Jesus, Marc was naturally sharing his faith and reaching out to others.

During my first five years as a believer, I never read a single book about incarnational outreach or relational evangelism. I simply spent time with people who were far from God, loved them with all the strength God gave me, and tried to let the presence of Jesus shine through. To my delight, many of them became Christians and also began reaching out to others in organic ways.

Outreach can be natural for all of us. One of the keys is to make sure we stay connected in relationships with people who are not believers. In Bill Hybels and Mark Mittelberg's book *Becoming a Contagious Christian*, the term *close proximity* describes this commitment to keep our lives intersecting with people who are spiritual seekers. To impact those who are far from God, we must come close to them in Jesus' name, making time for them, opening our hearts to them, and seeking to love them as Jesus does.

It's not all that complicated.

Theologians use the term *incarnation* to describe God's coming into human history. God left the glory of heaven and took on human flesh; Jesus was the incarnation of divinity who walked this earth. God came near. He was Immanuel—God with us.

Now we walk the earth as his ambassadors (2 Cor. 5:20), reflecting his light, love, and presence wherever we go. We seek to be like Jesus and to bring his presence, with the help of the Holy Spirit, into each situation we enter. We call this *incarnational living*.

Engaging the Cultural Landscape

The first step in bringing Jesus' presence into our world is learning to jump into our community with enthusiasm. We are not to fear and hate the world but to love it the way God does (John 3:16). This does not mean we are blind to the dangers of sin or temptation. Rather, it means that we explore and engage in our culture in loving and redemptive ways. This was the way of Jesus. He attended parties, ate dinner with sinners, hung out with prostitutes, touched lepers, embraced outcasts, got along with the wealthy, conversed with the religious elite, and enjoyed spending time with a diverse cross-section of humanity. There was no part of the cultural landscape Jesus did not travel.

Unfortunately, too many followers of Jesus run from the world and avoid cultural connections. If we are going to love and serve people, we need to learn how to engage with enthusiasm.

We should begin by taking some practical steps to connect regularly with people in our community. A friend of mine is a pastor at a church called Vintage Faith in Santa Cruz, California.[23] One of the things I love about Dan is that he immerses himself in the community of Santa Cruz. One weekend when I was preaching at a church in Santa Cruz, Dan and I decided to hang out for the evening. As we drove to a restaurant, Dan talked about the city, the people, the joys, and the challenges. It was obvious to me that he loves the town and the people who live there. As he pointed out places of interest, I noticed that each one was connected to a name, a person, a life. Most of the people Dan talked about were not yet followers of Jesus, but he was their friend and loved each one of them. My time with Dan inspired me to raise the bar on my own commitment to explore and engage in the community where God has planted me.

Brian is another friend who models a passionate heart for the world. He lives out an incarnational ministry in a natural way. Brian served as a missionary in Amsterdam for over a decade. He led one of the largest and most dynamic Christian churches in that part of the Netherlands. When people visited from the United States, they often commented on the legalization of prostitution in parts of Amsterdam and the fact that certain drugs can be purchased in the coffee shops. I always enjoyed watching Brian respond to their comments. He was gentle but firm as he shared his own perspective on Amsterdam.

Brian would talk about the honesty of the Dutch people and their lack of hypocrisy. He would speak of the beauty of the city, the needs of the people, and God's love for Amsterdam. Brian was immersed in the lives of people, engaged in effective ministry, in love with the culture, and quick to bless the city of Amsterdam. He was also profoundly aware of the challenges, struggles, and sins that gripped the city, but those were not his primary focus. Brian chose to walk among the people of Amsterdam as a friend. He had mastered the trains and the tram system, knew the culture, understood the people, and seemed as European as anyone else living there. No one was likely to guess that this international Christian pastor came from New York City and had been raised in the Jewish faith. Brian was living out an incarnational ministry that was an authentic and organic reflection of his love for Jesus and the people of Amsterdam.

I am so thankful that both Amsterdam and Santa Cruz are places where committed Christians have been called to live, minister, and reveal the presence and love of Jesus. Like every city of the world, these places are mission fields. To serve in these cities, someone has to love the people, enter into the culture, and incarnate the presence of Jesus.

So where has God placed you?

Your community, city, or village needs missionaries. Like Amsterdam and Santa Cruz, your community has unique needs and God is looking for Christ followers who will fearlessly enter into the culture and reveal the power and grace of God.

Removing ourselves from the people and criticizing the culture won't help. We can't run from the world and expect those same people to come to our churches. Instead, we are called to incarnate God's message of grace by making space in our lives and our schedules and finding ways to connect with people in our community who are not part of God's family.

A few years ago I felt I was becoming disconnected from the people in my community and decided to find ways to spend more time with people who are far from God. I quit the church soccer team and signed up for an open league at the indoor Soccer Spot. In a matter of weeks, I was getting to know about a dozen guys from all over our community and from numerous national backgrounds. One guy was a lapsed Jehovah's Witness from Vietnam. We connected immediately. My wife and I began inviting some of the team members over to our house after the games. That simple but intentional decision launched me into a new way of engaging with people in my community. It doesn't require much thought or creativity to find ways to open doors to new relationships and connections if we are willing to make an effort.

Two Warnings

As we prepare to engage our culture, I want to offer two brief but important words of caution. First, *be aware of the temptation to engage in cultural voyeurism.* Some Christians connect with the culture under the guise of reaching out, but in reality they are satisfying a sinful desire to gaze on the things of the world. I realized this during one of my trips to the Netherlands. Over the years, I have done a lot of training and teaching in Europe and have been to Amsterdam on many occasions. The first three times I was there, people asked me, "Have you been to the Red-Light District?" They explained that a lot of the Christians who visit go there to see "how bad things are." In this area of Amsterdam, prostitution and some drugs are legal, and women are displayed erotically in shop windows as objects to be purchased.

After my third invitation to visit the Red-Light District and my third "no thanks," I paused to think about what was happening. I had declined the offer to go observe the prostitutes because it just felt wrong to me. And as I reflected on it, it struck me that there was really nothing redemptive in going to see the Red-Light District. I knew it would just plant images and thoughts in my mind that ultimately would be unhelpful. For me, visiting the Red-Light District would have been nothing more than cultural voyeurism. As Christians who seek to interact meaningfully in our culture, we should occasionally stop to check our motives to make sure we are not engaging our culture on an unhealthy level.

Cultural voyeurism can include some less obvious activities as well. Many professing Christians watch movies and television shows that are quite raw and morally inappropriate. They try to justify their behavior by saying, "I just watch this stuff so I can stay up on what's happening in the culture." Some people visit websites to view provocative images and then defend their actions by saying, "I need to know what is happening in the world"; in truth, they are perfectly aware that these sites are inappropriate and unhealthy. Others might choose to hang out in bars or places on the fringes of society with the hope of reaching out, but they live with the secret that being in these places meets dark and sinful desires deep in their hearts.

If you are trying to engage the people in your culture but are being driven by impure motives, it's time to extricate yourself from places and activities that dishonor God. With this warning in mind, we also must be prepared to go where God leads us, even if he calls us to dark and difficult places. If our hearts and motives are pure, and we know that we can be there as salt and light, then our presence can be entirely appropriate. We must always use wisdom and continually examine our motives as we engage in different cultural situations.

A second warning is to *make sure you are influencing people and the culture with the truth of the gospel and not letting the cultural gravity pull you into behavior that dishonors God*. When my new friend Marc invited me to attend parties, I was confident I wouldn't be pulled into the behaviors that were prevalent at these gatherings, and by God's grace I was not. But if I had been tempted, the wise choice would have been to stay away.

Sherry and I made sure we taught this concept to our sons as they were growing up. All three of our boys attended public schools, had lots of friends who were not believers, and spent much of their time in homes and situations where they faced challenges to their faith. We knew our boys saw things that stretched them, heard things they didn't hear at home, and received invitations to participate in sinful activities. We taught them to stay in these friendships and situations as long as they could continue to be an influence for Jesus. But when they began to feel overwhelmed by the temptation to take part in wrong behavior, they were to remove themselves from the situation immediately. This same counsel is helpful to adult believers who are committed to being in the world but not of it.

If we are going to be like Jesus, we will engage in this world and be part of the culture around us. We won't run away. But if we are being sucked into sinful behavior, we should step back for a time until we are sure that we are influencing others and not being influenced *by* others in ways that are harmful to our spiritual growth. Also, we should honestly evaluate our motives and make sure we are exploring the culture for the sake of ministry and not to satiate the sinful desires of our hearts. When we have the right motive, our engagement in the world around us will reflect the heart of Jesus and lead to organic outreach.

Learning to Listen

Jesus listened to people. He not only heard their words, he cared about them inside and out. He didn't see people as projects. They were the object of his love.

Many people looked at a hated tax collector and saw only a traitor and a thief. Jesus looked at Matthew and saw a man who would become his friend and one of his inner circle of followers (Matt. 9:9).

The townspeople shunned the Samaritan woman, and she kept as far away from them as she could. She was seen as a relational and moral failure—a pariah to be avoided. But Jesus wanted to talk with her, to hear her heart, and to offer her living water (John 4:4). He became her friend and then her Lord.

Jesus had a habit of listening and relating to people right where they were. His life is a powerful example for those who desire to reveal God's presence in this world. Dr. Charles Van Engen, in his book *You Are My Witnesses*, writes, "Once we have begun to notice, listen to, and make ourselves available for our neighbor, we can begin to understand our neighbor more completely. Notice that relational evangelism does not begin with speaking—it begins with *listening*. And it may take a very significant amount of time and attention to listen well before we have won the right to speak."[24] What a concise reminder! Jesus listened and we must learn to do the same.

Followers of Christ should learn to listen as we encounter people face-to-face in our daily interactions, but we should also listen to the messages of our culture and the global community. We are wise to tune in to the conversations that are taking place on local, national, and global levels. I was reminded of this need when my friend Brian Newman came to preach at the church I was serving at some time ago. In his ministry in Amsterdam, Brian had learned to listen to the messages being communicated on a global level.

During the worship service, Brian showed a series of picture postcards submitted to a website that allows people to tell a secret anonymously.[25] I have used this same illustration a number of times since then and have updated my collection of postcards each time. One message that comes through this website loud and clear is "I am hurting." Here are a few of the messages on these postcards (submitted by real people):

- "I still believe my childhood bear is real. I am in college. I still talk to her ... when no one is in the room."
- "I pretend to be talking to someone on my cell phone ... but I'm really only talking to myself."
- On one postcard showing a woman who has dramatic body piercings is the message: "Everyone thinks I do it to make people stare ... but really, it's to keep them from looking too closely."

- "I am homeless and no one (not even my family) knows it."
- "I was sexually molested at the age of eight. I never told anyone. I'm forty-eight now. Thank you."
- "I may smile at older people but I'm thinking, 'Why are you alive and my parents are not?'"
- On a postcard with a picture of a giant hand holding tiny little babies is the secret: "I was pro-life before I had it done. I'm still pro-life after it."
- "Sometimes I hope the drugs will take me away before the loneliness ever gets its chance."
- "I miss feeling close to God."

As we listen to the themes and messages of the world, we learn how to respond with love. As we walk closely with people and hear their dreams, joys, fears, and worries, we get to know them as they really are. Too often followers of Jesus forget to listen. We are quick to point out what's wrong and tend to focus on the sin in the world. We sometimes stand in condemnation before we really get to know people's stories. We can be judgmental and harsh in moments when people need a listening ear and a warm embrace.

This is not to say that we should avoid disagreements or hold back from speaking words of correction. But if we fail to listen to people's stories, we are not going to have the authentic relational connection we need to truly impact them with God's words of grace.

Jesus listened and he loved. Sometimes he responded to what he heard with tender grace. At other times he gave strong words of challenge and conviction. But his words always came out of a deep knowledge of people and a profound understanding of their actions and the motives that drove them. As we listen to others, our understanding will grow and we will more accurately incarnate the presence of Jesus.

Making Space for People

Jesus lived with balance in his life. He made time to be alone with the Father, even when he was busy (Mark 1:35). He was careful to make space to train and equip his followers for ministry. He taught the masses as he traveled and preached. Yet he was always available to connect with the broken, the outcast, and the spiritually hungry. He made space for people in his schedule. He didn't see them as a disruption or an annoyance, but as the very reason he came to this earth.

Have you ever studied the Gospels just to take note of how often Jesus was interrupted? Over and over again, whether Jesus was traveling, resting, or teaching, he was surrounded by the pressing needs of other people. Frequently someone came looking for a healing, a blessing, a prayer for deliverance, an answer to a question, or a response to a concern. Jesus never seemed bothered and never treated people like interruptions. Instead, he made space for them.

"Jesus, bless our children." He stopped and blessed (Luke 18:15–16).

"Jesus, have mercy on me!" He opened blind eyes (Luke 18:38–43).

"Jesus, my servant is sick and suffering." He said the word and restored him (Luke 7:2–10).

"Jesus, have pity on us." He spoke and leprous skin was cleansed (Luke 17:12–14).

"Jesus, deliver my demon-possessed daughter." He healed her that hour (Matt. 15:22–28).

Even when a man was lowered through a ceiling in the middle of a message Jesus was delivering in a home meeting, he didn't seem fazed (Luke 5:19). Jesus simply forgave his sins and healed his body. These are just a few examples of times when Jesus was right in the middle of something and stopped what he was doing to minister to people in need.

How do we see the people in our lives? Do we look at them as interruptions or as divine appointments? Do we order our lives in a way that enables us to respond when needs arise? In her book *Listening for God*, Marilyn Hontz wisely writes, "Invite God to interrupt you. If your heavenly Father wanted to, could he interrupt you at any time during your day to ask you to do something with him?"[26] If we are to bring the presence and Spirit of Jesus to this world, we must make space, daily, for those who are broken, lonely, hurting, and outcast.

Making space for others can be done formally and informally. We make space by scheduling time to serve at a shelter, visiting people in jail, going on a mission trip, or volunteering for a service opportunity. But we also can make space for others in the normal flow of life. My friend Randy Frazee, in his book *Making Room for Life*, gives all kinds of ideas for ordering our days so that we have room for all we need to do, including being available to those who are far from God.[27] One simple idea he offers is to sit in front of your house with no particular agenda. If you have a porch, perfect. If not, a couple of lawn chairs will do the job. Just make yourself available and see who God brings to you.

Jesus actually seemed to enjoy it when people showed up unannounced. We can adopt this same attitude in our lives by asking God to help us slow down and make room for people. We can also seek to adopt a Christlike attitude when surprise visitors drop in and unexpected needs arise. As we respond in love, we reveal that Jesus is still available each time someone cries out, "Lord, have mercy on me!"

Sacrificial Living

Jesus sacrificed everything to reach out to us and purchase our salvation. His coming to this earth demanded a radical emptying of himself for our sake (Phil. 2:1–11). In his lifetime, he was rejected, abandoned by friends, abused, and arrested under false pretenses. He washed his followers' feet, one of the lowest forms of service in his day, to show them what a true disciple of Christ looks like (John 13:1–17). When he was arrested, Jesus could have stopped the entire ordeal with a snap of his fingers, calling upon the angels of heaven to rescue him (Matt. 26:53). But he didn't. While Jesus was hanging on the cross and pouring out his lifeblood for our sins, the people continued to mock him (Luke 23:36). At any point he could have said, "These people are not worth the sacrifice." Instead, Jesus bore our shame and carried our sins in his body on the cross. He died in our place, paying the ultimate price to redeem us (1 Peter 2:24).

Before Jesus went to the cross, he told his followers, "If anyone would come after me, he must deny himself and take up his cross daily and follow me" (Luke 9:23). If our outreach is to become more than just a fad of the month, it will require a willingness to make sacrifices. Martin Luther writes, "No tree bears fruit for its own use. Everything in God's will gives itself." Incarnating the presence of Jesus where we live will involve giving of ourselves, even when it hurts.

For many of us, our practical understanding of the Christian faith has eliminated the call to suffer and sacrifice. We like to have God's favor, his blessing, his good gifts, and an abundant life. But we don't like the idea of paying a price for these things. Gary Thomas, in his brilliant book *The Beautiful Fight*, ponders why many believers fail to see the world-changing impact of Christ in their lives. He writes, "Perhaps one of the reasons we so feebly bear the marks of Christ's promised transforming work in our lives is that we refuse to pay such a heavy price. We want to be delivered from our *troubles* instead of being delivered from our *sin*. We want to be like our affluent neighbor instead of like our rich Savior."[28] If we are unwilling to pay the price and embrace a sacrificial lifestyle, we will never experience the full extent of Christ's transforming power in our lives.

If we want to be salt and light in this world and bring the presence of Jesus into our homes and communities, we must choose to serve those in need and sacrifice whenever we can. We must be willing to suffer for the sake of the gospel out of love for people who might not even notice or bother to thank us.

What sacrifice can you make today? Who can you serve who might not ever be able to return the favor? How can you and I invite Jesus into our daily lives as we gladly suffer for those who need to see God's grace revealed to them? Answering these questions will help us discover how to be incarnational and organic in our outreach.

Overflowing Joy

Jesus was a model of joy. He had a passion for life that was contagious. He was never scolded for being too serious, but he was accused of enjoying parties and spending too much time with rowdy people (Matt. 9:11; 11:19). In her classic book on evangelism, *Out of the Saltshaker and into the World*, Rebecca Pippert tells about an awakening she experienced while reading the Gospels and seeking to learn more about Jesus. She writes, "My first impression was that Jesus is utterly delightful. He enjoyed people. He liked to go to parties and weddings. He was the kind of man people invited to dinner. And he came."[29] Jesus overflowed with joy.

As followers of Jesus who want to incarnate his presence in this world, we should exude the joy of the Lord. Of all the people on the face of the earth, Christians should be the ones who radiate joyful and true contentment. Through faith in Jesus we have a stockpile of blessings that reaches to heaven. Meditate for a moment on just a few of the good things God gives us when we receive his only Son as our Savior:

- Our sins are washed away (1 Cor. 6:11).
- We are friends of God (John 15:13–15).
- The Spirit of God dwells in us (John 14:17).
- Heaven belongs to us (Phil. 3:20).
- We are secure in God's hands (John 10:28–29).
- We have the fellowship of God's people, the church (1 John 1:7).
- We are given gifts of the Spirit (1 Cor. 12:7–11).
- We have the fruit of the Spirit growing in us (Gal. 5:22–23).

The list could go on for the rest of the book.

In my book *Seismic Shifts*, I look at small changes that can make a big difference in the life of a believer.[30] I spend the first three chapters of the book focusing on shifts that can bring greater joy than we have ever dreamed, because joy should be a central theme in the lives of believers. God wants us to live and walk in joy, and he wants the world to see it. Sometimes the best thing we can do for the world is to have a good time—for God's sake!

The world should look at Christians and be blown away by our love for life, our laughter, the brightness of our smiles, and the joy that overflows from our lives, homes, and churches. People should be drawn to our lives, and through them to Jesus, because the joy they see is magnetic. The apostle Paul puts it this way: "Rejoice in the Lord always. I will say it again: Rejoice!" (Phil. 4:4). Paul wrote these words while sitting in jail for telling others about Jesus. His example should serve as a reminder that true joy is not about avoiding suffering or the struggles of life. We will face hard times as we travel through this life, but we can always rejoice in the Lord regardless of our circumstances, because we find our hope in him.

Some believers run from the world and avoid engagement in culture, but this is not the way of Jesus. He left the glory of heaven to walk upon this earth; he connected with people from every walk of life and loved them deeply. His example calls us to engage intimately with people and to listen with open ears to those around us and to the voice of our culture. Make space in your daily schedule for those who are far from God, and be ready to sacrifice whatever it takes to bring God's love to this broken world. And finally, don't forget to let his joy fill you to overflowing. These are the patterns that reveal the way of Jesus and his presence to those around us.

Organic Activity: I Can Do That!

- *Listen Up*. In the coming week, take time to listen to people who are not Christians. What are their common fears, worries, passions, and dreams? As you listen, reflect on how God might meet them right where they are. As you begin to get a picture of what is on the hearts and minds of spiritually disconnected people, let it guide your prayers and the conversations you have with them.

- *Make Space*. If weather permits, spend at least fifteen minutes sitting in front of your house, apartment, or condo this week (if you live in a place where you have neighbors). As you sit, ask God to help you begin conversations and connect you to new people. Make space, be available, and see what happens!

- *Count Your Blessings*. As you seek to raise your joy quotient, make a list of some of the blessings you have in Christ. Use the list in the "Overflowing Joy" section of this chapter to get you started. Meditate on these blessings, thank God for them, and let your joy overflow so that others will see the goodness of God and long for the great things found in Jesus Christ.

- *Learn from Interruptions*. Study the gospels of Matthew, Mark, Luke, and John and take note of how Jesus responded to interruptions in the flow of his life.

Personal Reflection

- The apostle Paul boldly says, "Follow my example, as I follow the example of Christ" (1 Cor. 11:1). Would

I feel comfortable making this declaration? What aspects of my example would I *not* want others to follow? What can I do to change this?

- How can I change my weekly schedule to make more time and space to explore my community and develop new relationships with nonbelievers?
- How do I handle "interruptions"? How might I respond better to them?

Group Reflection

- Gary Thomas says that God gets glory "as we become walking billboards that proclaim his reality and redeeming power." What are some good messages that Christians announce through their "billboard" lives? What unhelpful messages might we be sending to the world, and how might we change the text on the billboards of our lives?
- Tell about a time you engaged in the world and felt that God used your presence to reveal his presence.
- What do you think about the two warnings given in this chapter when it comes to engaging and connecting in our culture?

  1. The warning to avoid cultural voyeurism.
  2. The warning to be careful that the world doesn't shape you but that your presence impacts the culture.

Prayer Direction

God of the manger, you came to our turf and lived as one of us. You did not fear the world but loved it. Teach me to engage with people and immerse myself in my community. Protect me from pitfalls and temptations that come with walking in this world. Help me to be like Jesus and bring his grace, joy, and love to my generation. I can do this only as you dwell in me. Fill me, Holy Spirit, and use me to show the world that Jesus lives, loves, and moves in this world. In his name, amen!

CHAPTER 9

Try SOMETHING

Part of outreach is taking action and having the courage to try new things. There is only one gospel, but there are many ways to express it and to reach people who are spiritually disconnected. Spirit-anointed creativity opens evangelistic doors as we try many ways to scatter the seed of the gospel.

Then he told them many things in parables, saying: "A farmer went out to sow his seed. As he was scattering the seed, some fell along the path, and the birds came and ate it up. Some fell on rocky places, where it did not have much soil. It sprang up quickly, because the soil was shallow. But when the sun came up, the plants were scorched, and they withered because they had no root. Other seed fell among thorns, which grew up and choked the plants. Still other seed fell on good soil, where it produced a crop—a hundred, sixty or thirty times what was sown. He who has ears, let him hear."

—Matthew 13:3–9

I like my way of doing evangelism better than your way of not doing it.

—D. James Kennedy,
Evangelism Explosion[31]

Because of exposure to unhealthy evangelism models, the evangelism enterprise has been hurt. Often it is the methodology of some of these models which offends the sensitivities of caring Christians. Sometimes they are artificial and unnatural.

—Joe Aldrich,
Lifestyle Evangelism

The articles and jokes just showed up on my desk—like magic. About once a month I'd come into my office and see the carefully cut pages filled with stories, illustrations, and jokes neatly stacked on the corner of my desk. Most of them related to farming in some way. They were consistently funny, and I kept many of them in my preaching files, just in case. One day Deb, one of the church custodians, asked me, "Do you like the jokes and stories my dad has been sending you?"

Mystery solved!

But the outreach adventure was just beginning.

For the past few months I had been praying for Deb's dad. Henry was a kind and gentle man, but he had been hurt by some Christians in his younger years and had written them all off (except his daughter). He had never set foot in a church building and was resistant to any talk of God and faith. He had a great sense of humor and for some reason had decided to serve me, a pastor he had never met, by sharing stories and jokes from his farming journals.

I asked Deb if she thought her dad would like to meet me. She was hesitant. "My parents have never had a pastor in their house. I don't know if he would be open to a visit." Instead of visiting, I decided to reciprocate Henry's kindness and started sending him articles, stories, and jokes from my walk of life—pastor stuff. I would always include a short handwritten note. For several months Henry and I exchanged packets of literature via our courier, Deb.

Just for the record, I had no plan, no program, and no three-steps approach to evangelistic success. I was just seeking the wisdom of the Spirit and praying for God's grace to reach Henry. I was trying something! I was throwing seed out there and praying it would find good soil.

One day Deb mentioned that her dad would like to meet me. This was a big step for him, and the best part was that he was the one who initiated it. We set a date and I dropped in to visit. Henry was warm, wise, funny, and an amazing storyteller. We talked freely and had a great visit. As long as nothing sounded or smelled like religion, we were fine. Over the coming months, we continued our sharing of literature and had occasional visits at Henry's place. In time he was willing to hear some of my story and was fascinated to learn how I came from a home with no faith. Our communication deepened as we shared more about our lives and loves, our joys and pains. The young pastor and the elderly hog farmer were becoming friends.

Then tragedy struck. Henry learned he had cancer. I was able to visit him occasionally, but some family members felt it would be good for Henry to have some space and requested that I stay away for a time. I knew Henry's health was failing, and I wanted so much to talk with him in greater depth about Jesus. But I wasn't able to visit him. For a time our relationship was placed on hold, but I continued praying and received regular updates from Deb.

As I got to know Henry, I learned that sharing God's love doesn't always come with clear instructions. Sometimes we just need to press on and try different things as we interact with people who are not yet followers of Jesus. We must be creative, tossing seeds freely and continually trying new ideas. When we bump into an obstacle, we just try something else—outreach can be quite experimental.

With Henry, the starting point of our relationship was sending each other stories and jokes. To be honest, I haven't used this approach since my time with Henry. Every person is unique, so each journey with a seeking friend will be different. Remember, outreach is an adventure, not a formula. It takes flexibility, creativity, and an adventurous heart.

Creativity: Try *Something*

What is the right way to reach out to a person who is living on the borderlands of faith? How do we connect in meaningful ways with those who have not yet received Jesus? Our answers to these questions will depend on the person—on their temperament, loves, struggles, history, and passions. Over the years, I have walked with many people as they have moved toward faith in Jesus, and I'm still traveling with a good number of them. Each journey has been different, requiring a Spirit-anointed creativity.

For those who like neat five-steps programs and proven formulas, this diversity can be a bit frustrating. Christians who are waiting to scatter seed when the soil looks rich, the conditions are perfect, and success is guaranteed may end up waiting a long time.

It is wiser to start scattering seed today and just see what happens—toss it out there!

"But what if the soil isn't ready?"

"What if I encounter resistance?"

"What if nothing happens?"

As long as you are spreading gospel seed and watering wherever you go, God will be honored. Your job is not to guarantee results but to scatter and water.

If you encounter a speaker or writer who claims that you *must follow* three, six, or eleven steps and people will automatically come to faith in Jesus, beware! Outreach is simply not that simple. It can be messy, and it is often risky. It involves faith that God really is working, even when we can't see results. Evangelism is not about a magic formula. It is about the power of God and the faithfulness of his people, people like you and me. We scatter the seed, but he brings the growth (1 Cor. 3:6).

Of course some general rules, principles, and approaches can be helpful. But locking yourself into an inflexible program can be counterproductive. Every evangelistic encounter poses new dynamics, challenges, and joys. The key is not finding the perfect program but learning to toss seed *wherever* we go.

In many ways, doing outreach is like trying on new clothes. Before making a clothing purchase, most people will try on a shirt, a pair of pants, or some other piece of clothing to see how it fits. If the clothing is too tight or too loose, they'll try another size. If the color or style really does not work for them, they may put it back on the rack. When buying clothes, we often try several options to see what works.

Outreach is often like that. We try something to see how it goes. If it feels organic, we wear it! If it just doesn't fit well, we try something else. We continue trying new things until we find a way of reaching out that we can "wear," a way that shows off our love for Jesus and our faith in God.

Facing Obstacles and Taking Risks

As I entered into a relationship with Henry, I knew there would be obstacles. Don't be alarmed—obstacles are normal. I remember asking Deb if she thought her dad would come to a church event. She chuckled kindly and replied, "No way!"

So I tried another option: "Would he be open to my dropping in for a visit?"

"I don't think so—not yet," was her reply.

Strike two.

That's when it hit me. Since Henry had been sending *me* stuff through Deb, maybe I could return the favor and send *him* some literature.

Bingo! That was the next step—finding a way past the obstacles.

Notice that I bumped into a couple of roadblocks before finding a connecting point with Henry that would be natural for both of us. Later, when I began visiting with Henry, there was a whole new set of obstacles. Could I share Jesus using a confrontational approach? No way! Henry had been hurt by overbearing Christians in the past. This tactic would slam the door shut and reinforce negative stereotypes. What about encouraging him to read a book on apologetics? While this would be a great connection point for some people, Henry was not really asking those kinds of questions. What seemed organic in this situation was simply continuing our habit of sharing stories and jokes. We talked about life. Since I'm a Christian, this would come up as I shared my journey. It was natural for me to talk about my faith at times. At this stage in our friendship, there were still some obstacles to sharing Jesus, but I found my way around them and persisted in getting to know Henry.

I knew that any time I tried to raise spiritual issues, Henry would be resistant. But I was willing to take that risk. Jesus is my closest friend, and my faith permeates every part of my life. So how can I have an honest friendship filled with many conversations about life and avoid talking about my faith?

Will there be roadblocks when we begin naturally sharing our faith with nonbelievers? Of course! Will we face risks as we learn to connect on a deeper level and invite the spiritual dynamic of life into our conversations? We can count on it. But these are small risks to take compared with the joy of seeing Jesus touch a human heart.

Some Ideas and Reflections

I won't even try to offer you a program for getting past roadblocks and avoiding risks. You will have to go through that process on your own. But I can tell you this: if you love people and spend time listening for the leading of the Holy Spirit, you will find your way. I coach a group of about forty leaders in the discipline and practice of evangelism. In my coaching, I never tell them what to do or how to relate to the unbelievers in their lives. Instead, I repeatedly encourage them to spend time regularly with their friends and family members who are not yet believers, to pray a lot, and to follow the Spirit's direction. It amazes me, over and over again, as I hear story after story of how God gave them an organic approach that fit their unique situation and personality. Often they end up sharing their faith in a way they never would have come up with on their own.

Though there is no set program for evangelism, there are many different approaches we can learn that can be quite helpful as we walk with people who live on the borders of faith. You'll notice that all of these ideas have a relational dynamic. As you seek the Lord's leading in your relationships with lost people, these are just a few of the approaches you could try.

"COME WALK WITH ME"

Invite people to join you in the regular activities of your life. If your faith is real, it will shine through in the way you live. Don't think primarily of church programs or overtly faith-based activities. Just invite people to be with you as you walk through life each day. You could extend an invitation to go shopping, go out to lunch, spend time cooking together, attend a sporting event, go on vacation, or pick out a new lawn mower. You can do just about anything, but make sure that you bathe this time in prayer. When you get together, just be yourself. Don't force religious conversations, but when your faith comes up as an organic part of your life, don't be embarrassed about it or hold back. Let people see that your relationship with Jesus is a normal part of who you are—in every area of life.

HOSTING MATTHEW PARTIES

In the New Testament, we read that Matthew had a party and invited all his new friends (Jesus and the disciples) and all his old friends (tax collectors, prostitutes, and sinners) over for dinner one evening (Matt. 9:10).[32] The picture is beautiful—two worlds coming together. Believers and nonbelievers share a meal, rub shoulders, and connect.

Too many Christians compartmentalize their lives and keep their "church friends" away from their "other friends." By making a point of pulling together our Christian and non-Christian friends, we open the door for God to work. When these worlds meet, people who are far from God can discover that Christians are just normal people. (That's assuming your Christian friends are normal.) These moments create opportunities for new friendships to be forged. They are great times to start interesting conversations. A "Matthew party" is a time for followers of Jesus to let different worlds intersect and see what happens.

LEARNING TOGETHER

There are some people you will encounter who tend to *think* their way through life instead of *feeling* their way around issues. These folks love to learn and might be open to exploring the questions of faith if you are willing to take time to dig in with them.

Rudy had not grown up going to church, and he still carried some scars in his heart because he had been rejected by his "Christian" neighbors as a young boy. It seems that Rudy's dad had committed an unpardonable sin in the eyes of his highly religious neighbors. He mowed the lawn on Sundays. In responding to his "sin," many of the neighborhood parents told their children they couldn't play with Rudy. This experience pushed Rudy away from the church and closed him off to Christians for many years.

When I met Rudy, he was asking lots of questions about God and had even started reading the Bible. He had a notebook full of questions about the Christian faith. Rudy was a computer programmer, and he wanted to understand the details and fill in all the blanks. I came to appreciate Rudy's sharp mind and his passion for learning. The most natural way for us to connect was to study together.

We met for several weeks and had interesting conversations that covered such diverse topics as theology, the Bible, football, computer programming, parenting, and our favorite fast-food restaurants. Rudy had some keen insights into Scripture, and he felt free to ask any question that came to mind. I certainly didn't have all the answers, but together we dug in and found many of the answers to Rudy's questions about God. After weeks of study, I asked Rudy, "Are you at a place where you can put your trust in Jesus and ask him to forgive you and lead your life?"

He looked at me and said, "I don't know. This is huge. This decision is even bigger than getting married or having children. This is the most important decision of my life."

I agreed and asked Rudy if he was ready to make life's biggest commitment and step across that line of faith.

He paused and said, "I need more time. I'm not ready yet."

The next week, when Rudy walked in the door, I saw a glow on his face and a bounce in his step. Something was different. We chatted for a few minutes until I finally asked, "So what's up—where are you with this whole Jesus thing?" He said with confidence, "I'm ready! What do I need to do?" I told him that he needed to talk to Jesus in prayer and tell him what was on his heart. We had already walked through the gospel several times over the past couple of months, so I knew he understood the message. That day, Rudy confessed his sins, received Jesus, and entered God's family. His journey to the point of recognizing his need for forgiveness and embracing faith involved an extended time of study with a friend who patiently welcomed his questions. Some of the people you know may also need to travel down this road.

PROVIDING CHRISTIAN RESOURCES

Some people won't want to sit and study with you but will be open to listening to a CD, watching a DVD, reading a book, or visiting a website. They too are learners, but they prefer more space to work through things on their own.

My brother Jason was like this. He has a sharp mind and loves to weigh options and reflect on various perspectives. While he was investigating the Christian faith, people gave him several books and tapes. He read classics like C. S. Lewis's *Mere Christianity,* Josh McDowell's *Evidence That Demands a Verdict,* and Lee Strobel's *Case for Christ.* The Christians in his life who cared about him consistently provided solid resources and kept the door open for conversation whenever Jason wanted to talk. Over time, as he studied these resources, read through the Bible, and opened his life to the work of the Holy Spirit, Jason came to the point where he was ready to embrace Jesus with both his mind and his heart.

Many helpful resources are available for Christians to pass on to their seeking friends. In the Recommended Resources section in the back of this book I have included book titles and web addresses that might be helpful as you provide resources to people who are exploring the Christian faith.

INVITING OTHERS TO CHURCH-BASED GATHERINGS

So often we think of inviting people to a church service as our main goal when we are reaching out. I believe this is a mistake. Don't get me wrong—I'm all for inviting people to worship services, but often it's best to establish a relationship with them and share a bit of life together first. When the time is right, however, it can be a wonderful thing to invite your unbelieving friends to church—if your church service will be relevant for them.

In the meantime, there are all sorts of other opportunities, besides a church service, to extend an invitation. Take a look at what happens at your church (or at church-sponsored events) throughout the week, and think about who you might invite to come with you. My first time at church with my sister, over thirty years ago, wasn't a church service but a game night for students. After the game night, I went on a church-sponsored water skiing trip with students from the church. I'll share more about this in part 3 of this book, but in my journey to faith, a number of my initial contacts with God came at some rather unconventional church-sponsored events, not at Sunday morning worship services.

Over the past few years, I have learned of all sorts of events that can be natural connection points for spiritual seekers, including music and choral programs, church dinners and picnics, summer children's programs like vacation Bible school, special Christmas and Easter programs, euchre nights, wild game dinners (where people cook and eat fish they have caught and meat they have hunted), square dances, concerts, recovery programs, financial help seminars ... the list goes on and on.

The key is to look at the events and programs your church offers and identify something that happens at your church (or with your friends from church) that looks like a natural fit for an unchurched friend. Then say a prayer and invite them. If your friend comes, the door is opened for meaningful connections and ongoing spiritual conversations.

Serving Others

Jesus modeled humble service and then called his followers to learn from his example. In John 13 we read about Jesus washing the feet of his disciples. In the teaching that followed this shocking action, Jesus asked his disciples, " 'Do you understand what I have done for you? You call me "Teacher" and "Lord," and rightly so, for that is what I am. Now that I, your Lord and Teacher, have washed your feet, you also should wash one another's feet. I have set you an example that you should do as I have done for you. I tell you the truth, no servant is greater than his master, nor is a messenger greater than the one who sent him. Now that you know these things, you will be blessed if you do them' " (vv. 12–17).

Every act of service by a follower of Jesus shows the world that Jesus is alive and active in this world. As we follow Jesus' example and serve others, we model his love and compassion.

The Thirty-Seconds Rule

The Thirty-Seconds Rule is a commitment to pause at specific times in the flow of a day to recalibrate our hearts and eyes toward the people around us. It's a time to allow the Holy Spirit to tune us in to *what* he would have us do and *who* he would have us love. It's a chance to say to God, "Here I am. I'm ready to scatter the seed of your gospel. Please use me as a conduit of your living water to help seed grow." When we hit the pause button on our day, the whole direction of our lives can change. The Thirty-Seconds Rule is so simple anyone can do it. In the course of your day, just make time to stop for thirty seconds and ask these three simple questions.

1. What would the Spirit of God prompt me to pray as I walk into this portion of my day?
2. Who does God want me to notice right now?
3. How might I extend the love of God and the grace of Jesus in this situation?

Ordinary people who establish a pattern of taking thirty seconds to listen and respond to God will find their lives moving in new directions. Here are some natural times to pause and implement the Thirty-Seconds Rule:

• Walking into your workplace or school.
• Entering the home of someone who is not yet a follower of Jesus.
• Engaging in a social setting that involves people who are far from God.
• Walking into a restaurant, store, or other business.
• Driving down the street where you live.
• Entering any place you go on a daily basis.

The Thirty-Seconds Rule is simply a decision to take your foot off the emotional gas pedal of your day and slow down enough to let the Holy Spirit sensitize your heart to what is happening around you.

Every single day we have many opportunities to extend grace, share God's love, and care for the people we encounter. But too often we race past these open doors. Practicing the Thirty-Seconds Rule creates open moments for God to speak and offer direction.

One afternoon my wife, Sherry, and I took a walk around our neighborhood. We didn't have plans to "do ministry" or "reach out" to neighbors. We were just taking a walk. But as we walked, we talked about how much we love our neighbors (those who are committed Christians and those who haven't yet embraced Jesus). As we came back to our street, I noticed that a lot of garage doors were open. It was spring, and after a long Michigan winter, people were finally coming out of hibernation. It was a perfect Thirty Seconds moment: pray, notice, take action.

To our delight, three of our neighbors were outside, and we had a chance to talk with them and deepen our relationships. The implementation of the Thirty-Seconds Rule led to about twenty minutes of connecting.

Another time, I was visiting some friends who have become very dear to me who are not followers of Jesus. As I pulled up in front of their house, I paused for thirty seconds. "God, I love these people so much. I want them to know your love, your amazing grace, and the plan you have for them. Please sensitize me to their needs. Let your love shine through. Give me both wisdom and boldness to know what to say and when to be silent. Here I am, Lord. Use me."

At that point, I had made myself available to God. Now I would wait on the Spirit for an open door. The couple I was visiting were old friends of our family, and over the years they had grown more and more open to spiritual things. But they also could get very defensive and close off if they felt like someone was trying to "push religion" on them. In a quiet moment the wife pulled me aside and shared that she was struggling with her husband's lack of motivation in life. She wondered what I thought it would take to stir his heart and give him meaning and purpose.

I immediately saw this moment as divinely orchestrated. I asked her, "Do you really want to know what I believe Ben needs to receive fresh direction in his life?" She assured me that she wanted to know my thoughts on the topic.

I shared my testimony of how my life had lacked direction and focus until I became a follower of Jesus. I told her how my life had dramatically changed after I accepted Christ and asked him to forgive my sins and be the leader of my life. I told her that I believed the only way Ben would find power to set a new direction for his life was if he became a follower of Jesus.

Instead of becoming defensive and cutting off the conversation, she said, "Maybe that's what it will take—an act of God!"

I asked her, "Would you mind if I took a moment to pray for Ben—and for you?"

She said she would like that very much. So then and there I cried out to God for Nancy and Ben. Nancy sat beside me, praying with me to a God she didn't yet know, asking God to help her husband.

I am convinced that the open door for this powerful moment came during the thirty seconds I paused to ask God to open my eyes and use me.

Will you take thirty seconds, just a few times each day, to recalibrate your heart? If you are willing, God is ready to move in fresh and powerful ways.

This book includes many examples of ways we can scatter seed and let the living water of Jesus flow through us. We often don't know if the soil of people's hearts will be ready. And we must always remember that we can't change anyone. Our part is not to transform hearts; it's to spread the seed of the gospel liberally. So get started today! Throw some seed out there, try something new, and see what God does.

PLANTING AND WATERING

Organic Activity: I Can Do That!

- *Try the Thirty-Seconds Rule.* Identify one or two times in a normal day when you might pause to reorient your heart toward outreach. Over the next few days, use these moments to implement the Thirty-Seconds Rule.
- *"Come Walk with Me."* Who could you invite to "come walk with you" as you carry out some activity or responsibility in the coming week? How might God use this time to build a redemptive bridge in your relationship with this person?
- *Throw a Matthew Party.* Make plans in the coming month to get a group of friends together for a meal, a barbeque, a game night, or just a good old hangout time. Make sure you invite friends who are strong Christians as well as friends who have not yet embraced Christ as their Lord. Pray for God to build bridges, spark friendships, and move in people's hearts by his Spirit.

Personal Reflection

- What are some of the surprising and unique ways God used people to reach out to me and help me forward on my spiritual journey?
- What obstacles have I faced as I've tried to scatter seed and reach out in Jesus' name? What has helped me get past these roadblocks?
- Some people have established a specific evangelistic program or series of steps they believe a Christian can

use with all people in all situations. What are some potential pitfalls of this approach?

Group Reflection

- Recall the story about Henry in the introduction to this chapter. This story presents some unconventional approaches to outreach. Tell a story about a time God opened the door for you to connect with a nonbeliever through unique and surprising ways.
- In your efforts to scatter the seed of the gospel, what is one approach that just did not work for you? Why wasn't this approach a good fit?
- What is one way you have reached out that clicked and felt natural? Why do you think this approach fits you?
- What are some of the resources you might give a person who wants to learn more about the Christian faith?

Prayer Direction

Creator of the heavens and the earth, you are the ultimate artist. You are creative beyond measure. You have made each person beautiful and unique. If I am to be used by you in this world, I need to be infused with your creative energy. Give me boldness to try new things. Grant me grace when an outreach effort doesn't work and humility when it does. I know you want the seed of your gospel scattered all over the world. Here are my hands and my heart; use me for your glory. Amen.

PART 3

Bearing Kingdom Fruit

Every Christian has a story of coming to faith in Jesus Christ. This is mine.

I was born into a loving and healthy family but was raised with no formal religious allegiance or training. I remember going to church a few times when I was a little boy, but faith in Jesus was not taught in our home. We learned about morality and about being good people, but these ideas were rooted in an altruistic commitment to making the world a better place and not in any belief in a higher power or divine being who wanted to be involved in our lives. Growing up, I wasn't just unaware of the teachings of Christianity; I was raised in a religious vacuum. Faith was not taught at all in our family.

I can't recall any neighbors who went to church faithfully. Growing up in Orange County, California, during the 1960s and '70s, I lacked the strong cultural understanding of religion I might have received had I grown up in the Midwest.

I did know at least one "religious" family. The mother occasionally provided child care for me and my two older sisters. She was kind, but her husband was one of the meanest people I met in my childhood. I don't know what brand of Christian he was; I just knew he went to church, talked about God, and was flat-out mean. I can still remember the time he wrestled me to the ground and stuffed lima beans down my throat because I refused to eat them. I can't recollect the full text of the sermon he preached as he jammed the beans into my mouth, but it included lines about being thankful to God for what I had and appreciating food that people in Africa would have been glad to eat. Needless to say, his actions did nothing to endear me to the Christian faith.

When I was in third grade, a close friend died of leukemia. I talked to some adults and asked questions like, "What happens when a person dies?" "Where is David right now?" "What will happen when my life ends?" No one I talked to had any answers for me. One person I really respected even admitted, "I don't know what happens when a person dies." He then referred me to a seven-volume set of books on world religions and told me I could study these books and discover my own beliefs. Since I was only in the third grade, the idea of reading a couple thousand pages of small print written by scholars was not all that appealing. I figured that if these people didn't have answers, no one did. So I put my spiritual quest on pause. By the time I reached my high school years, I had absolutely no interest in spiritual things. They were nowhere on my radar.

When I was a sophomore, my sister Gretchen began going to a church youth group and eventually made a commitment to Jesus. I had no idea what it meant at the time, except that she started being really nice to me. I didn't know how to respond to her gestures of kindness, but I did know how to react to her invitations to come to her church group. I rejected them flatly and became even harsher and more abusive toward her.

One day Gretchen came to me with an offer that actually sounded interesting. She told me that her youth group would be holding a casino night and wondered if I wanted to come.[33] She said there would be roulette wheels, blackjack tables, and many other games. There would even be a twenty-girl can-can dancing line.

For the first time, church sounded interesting. So I went.

It was all true! The games ... the girls ... the gambling.

Now, I don't know if your church would find this kind of event appropriate for youth, but it was the only invitation to church that Gretchen gave (and she had given a lot of them) that I accepted. I had a great night, won some prizes, and met a cute blonde. I even heard a message about God. I think the title was "Life's a Gamble—Where You Puttin' Your Chips?" I heard about Jesus for the first time.

The next week I went back to the youth group. This week wasn't a casino night but just a regular group meeting. The reason I went back was simple—I had met a girl the week before. Over the next few months, I attended the group, hung out with the cute blonde, and started listening to the messages. I met some other high school students who seemed to care about each other and me. It wasn't too bad.

After a few months of attending this church youth group, I was invited to go on a week-long water skiing trip. We would be living on the water in houseboats. It sounded exciting, so I was in.

Before we arrived at the Sacramento River Delta area, it never occurred to me to wonder what it might mean to live on a houseboat for a week with a bunch of Christians. We were out floating on the water and I had no way to escape from them. Every day, they studied the Bible, sang songs, and talked about Jesus. The leaders on the boat, Gary and Doug, were great guys and very passionate about their faith. The other students and the college leaders were kind and never pushed me; they were just authentically excited about Jesus, and it showed. Every evening, a couple of people would tell their story about how they had became a follower of Christ.

As the week pressed on, my heart was growing softer. The messages the youth pastor back at the church had given over the past few months were starting to sink in. The Spirit of God was alive among the group on the boat, and he was starting to reach me as well. The love my sister was expressing to me, along with the servant-hearted care being extended by the college-age leaders from the church, really impressed me. Most of all, God was starting to break through my hard and resistant heart.

On the last day of the trip, one of the boat leaders shared the simple story of the gospel. He talked of the amazing love of God and how he cares about every person who walks this earth. He clearly addressed the issue of sin and said that all of us have offended God and rebelled against him. I remember thinking, "If there is a perfect God out there, I have done more wrong than most people." I had no problem identifying myself as a sinner. The leader went on to tell us about the consequences of sin: our separation from God, a death sentence, and the reality of eternal judgment. As strange as it might seem, these ideas made sense to me. With all my sins, I knew I deserved God's judgment.

But he also told us how Jesus came to this earth—God in human flesh. How he lived a perfect life and then died on the cross to pay for our sins. His resurrection three days later was the affirmation that Jesus was exactly who he said he was and that his shed blood was enough to wash us clean and give new life. God had done it all through Jesus. There was nothing we could do, no good works to add, no human effort to contribute. The work of my salvation was completed on the cross and in the reality of the empty tomb.

The boat leader went on to explain that God offers the gift of Jesus to anyone who believes in him and receives what he has done. "Just confess your sins, embrace Jesus, and watch what happens." There I was, at the moment of decision. The leader gently asked if anyone wanted to respond and receive Jesus.

I didn't have all the answers. I wasn't a Bible scholar. I had no religious background. I didn't even have a single verse of the Bible memorized. But my heart was open.

I can still remember my prayer that night. It went something like this: "Dear God, I don't know if you are really there, but if you are, I want to know you. I also don't know if all this stuff about Jesus is true, but if it is, and he died for me, I want him. I confess my sins, and I have lots of them. I ask Jesus to clean me up and give me a new life. God, if you can do something with my life, you can have it. Amen."

My prayer was not profound or theologically deep, but it was all I knew at the time. Three decades later I can say with unwavering confidence that Jesus forgave me that night, my sins were washed away, the Holy Spirit entered my heart, and I became a child of God.

Everything changed!

That same night, as I lay in my sleeping bag on top of the houseboat looking up at the stars, I heard God speak for the first time. I recognized his voice, though I had never heard it before. His words were clear and made perfect sense to me. "Kevin, spend the rest of your life telling people about Jesus, or you will be miserable." That might sound harsh, but it was exactly what I needed to hear. I knew few things at that point in my life, but I was confident that I did not want to be miserable. I responded, "Okay, God, I'm in."

The next morning I climbed down the ladder from the roof of the houseboat. The first person I saw was a volunteer leader from the church. I asked him, "What do I have to do to become a pastor?" He looked at me and laughed. Then he said, "Get a haircut." At the time my hair was well past my shoulders. Of course, he was just kidding about the hair. After a moment he realized I was serious, so he gave a more reflective response. He said, "It might be good if you graduated from high school." He knew I had a 0.75 GPA the past school year and that I was not on the fast track for graduation. We had a wonderful conversation about the need for me to adjust a number of habits and behaviors if I really wanted to be a pastor someday.

From that moment on, the course was set. God had called and I was ready to follow. I was a Christian, I was called to serve Jesus, and I was ready to do whatever it took to spend my life serving God.

So that's my story.

When people ask me, "How did a guy who grew up with no faith end up in the church serving as a pastor?" I tell them, "I went for the gambling, I stayed for the women, and I found Jesus."

That's my story, and I'm sticking to it.

God Loves Fruit

I know that my story of faith brings joy to God's heart, and so does yours! God celebrates every one of his children who comes home through faith in Jesus. When God invites you and me to go into the harvest fields of this world and enter into his love, he is asking us to share in the joy of *fruit bearing*.

Imagine telling a farmer to get the soil in his field ready for planting. You instruct him to sow lots of seeds and then to cover them with good soil. After that, you tell him he needs to water the seeds faithfully and consistently. Just before he leaves, you add one final piece of information: "Oh, and for the record, Farmer Joe, nothing will grow. That's right—no crops, not a single stalk of corn or head of wheat. There will be nothing to harvest. Be sure to have fun farming!"

How many people do you think would be motivated to get up early in the morning and work all day if they knew there was no hope of a harvest? The answer is obvious—none!

The work of a farmer is not easy. But good farmers work hard to prepare the soil, plant the seeds, water them, and keep the fields free from weeds, all for a very good reason—they anticipate the time of the harvest! They look forward to hauling in bushel baskets of fresh fruit and filling their barns full of crops.

As we engage in this amazing task of outreach, we can and should anticipate the harvest that will come. God is ready for our lives and our prayers to bear his kingdom fruit. Lives will be changed by the message of the gospel, and the hearts of men, women, and children will be transformed and healed for all of eternity when they place their faith in Jesus Christ. This is the vision Jesus painted for us when he spoke of the harvest, saying, "Still other seed fell on good soil. It came up and yielded a crop, a hundred times more than was sown" (Luke 8:8).

That's why we prepare the soil diligently, scatter the seed liberally, and water the ground faithfully. God has invited us to be part of his harvest—and God loves fruit!

CHAPTER 10

The Work of the HOLY SPIRIT

We can do our part, but only God can draw people to Jesus and change their lives. One essential element of sharing our faith is learning to listen for God's leading as we work in partnership with the Holy Spirit.

"But you will receive power when the Holy Spirit comes on you; and you will be my witnesses in Jerusalem, and in all Judea and Samaria, and to the ends of the earth."

—Acts 1:8

After they prayed, the place where they were meeting was shaken. And they were all filled with the Holy Spirit and spoke the word of God boldly.

—Acts 4:31

I'm more convinced than ever that the absolute highest value in personal evangelism is staying attuned to and cooperative with the Holy Spirit.... The only thing you need in order to sustain an effective approach to evangelism year after year after year is an ear fine-tuned to the prompting of the Holy Spirit.

—Bill Hybels,
*Just Walk across
the Room*

The Rest of the Story

In chapter 9 I told you part of my outreach journey with Henry, the kindhearted farmer whom I met by exchanging jokes and stories. Though he was resistant to the message of Jesus, we forged a wonderful friendship over time. Here is the rest of his story.

Henry was dying. The end was near, and I wanted so much to visit him. Since the family requested that guests not go to the hospital, I honored their wish. Instead, I prayed, along with many others, for God to break through to his heart. I also prayed for his daughter, Deb, a member of my church, to know how to love, serve, and share the gospel one more time with her dad. Eternity was hanging in the balance.

Then I got the call.

Henry had received Jesus. It was a mighty work of the Holy Spirit, yet another miracle in God's amazing redemptive history spanning the centuries. I shouldn't have been surprised, but I was. Many people had been praying for Henry. My wife, a friend of Deb's, had made a Holy Spirit–led commitment to pray for Henry's salvation every time she drove by his house. Though she had never met him, Sherry had prayed hundreds of times for his conversion over a nine-year period! When we got the news that Henry had received Jesus into his life, we lifted up our hearts and voices. We gave praise to the Father who loves us, the Son who gave his life for us, and the Holy Spirit who softens hearts of stone.

This is the report we received from Deb, Henry's daughter.

Deb had gone to her parents' house to spend the night with her mom. Henry was being treated at a local hospital with little hope of coming home again. Early in the morning, Deb was awakened by a clock that was chiming quite loudly. She thought it was a strange time for the clock to go off and asked her mom when they had gotten the clock fixed (it had been broken).

Her mother gave her a strange look. "That clock doesn't work, Deb. It's still broken," she said.

"Then why was it ringing so loud that it woke me up this morning?"

Deb's mother continued to insist that the clock was broken, and told Deb that she had not heard the clock make any sound at all.

Something in her heart told Deb that the Spirit of God was on the move and God was trying to get her attention. She decided to drive to the hospital right away to see her father. From the moment she walked into the room and looked at her dad, she could see that something had changed—Henry was a new man. He had a glow, and Deb could sense God's Spirit in him.

Henry turned to his daughter and said, "You don't have to worry about me anymore, Deb. Everything's okay." He explained that Jesus had come to see him that morning and had spoken to him. Henry had a vision and met Jesus face-to-face, and afterward he had made the decision to receive him as his Lord. As the details of the story unfolded, Deb began to realize that the timing of her father's meeting with Jesus coincided with the moment she had heard the clock chime at her parents' home. At that moment Henry had received forgiveness for his sins and entered God's family.

Within four days Henry had the opportunity to see Jesus a second time. The Good Shepherd came and brought Henry, his new sheep, to his heavenly home. I had the honor of performing the funeral service, which was a wonderful celebration of God's amazing grace and persistent love.

Every time I reflect on Henry's journey to Jesus, I am reminded that we can scatter seeds and we can water, but only God can change hearts—and often in unexpected, miraculous ways! Henry's story may be unusual, but every time a heart is changed and a person becomes a follower of Jesus, we celebrate a miracle of God's grace. God's Spirit was at work in Henry's life even when I could not visit. God actively answered prayers even while Henry's wife and daughter were at home sleeping. At the end of the day, I'm reminded that the work of salvation belongs to God alone as he moves in our lives by his Holy Spirit. We can do our part, but *only God saves people*.

No Credit

We don't get credit when someone comes to faith in Jesus. We also don't have to live with the blame if a person remains hard-hearted.

We have our work to do—clearly and faithfully communicating the message of the gospel. But God and God alone transforms hearts.

Outreach leaves no room for boasting about how we have "saved" people or about how many souls we have "won." Instead, we give all the praise and honor to Jesus. He is the one who died and rose again. Yes, the Spirit of God works through us, empowering us to present the message of Jesus, but only that same Spirit has the power to bring a person into a saving relationship with Jesus.

Robert Coleman, in his book *The Master Plan of Evangelism*, writes, "It is only the Spirit of God that enables one to carry on the redemptive mission of evangelism. Jesus underscored this truth early in relation to His own work by declaring that what He did was in cooperation with 'the Spirit of the Lord.' It was by His virtue that He preached the gospel to the poor, healed the brokenhearted, proclaimed deliverance to the captive, opened the eyes of the blind, cast out demons, and set at liberty those that were oppressed (Luke 4:18; Matthew 12:28)."[34]

Jesus taught his followers that partnership with the Spirit is essential—so essential that Jesus himself looked to the Spirit as he reached out. The apostle Paul puts it this way: "What, after all, is Apollos? And what is Paul? Only servants, through whom you came to believe—as the Lord has assigned to each his task. I planted the seed, Apollos watered it, but God made it grow. So neither he who plants nor he who waters is anything, but only God, who makes things grow" (1 Cor. 3:5–7). These words are not meant to diminish our part but are intended to put things in perspective. We can do our part in the outreach equation, but unless God intervenes and makes seeds grow, there will never be a harvest. We don't get the *credit* when a person comes to faith in Jesus. But we do get to share in the *joy* of the harvest.

No Blame

Some believers live with deep-seated guilt and anxiety when it comes to evangelism. They fear that all kinds of people will not be in heaven because they missed an opportunity to force a point of decision. These people may heap blame on themselves, but in some cases the blame is piled on them by others, people whose theology places the full responsibility for salvation on the work of the messenger.

I remember bumping into a young Christian man I had not seen since his wedding about a year earlier. I knew he felt a leading toward full-time Christian service, so I stopped to check in with him about his marriage and his dream of going into the ministry. As we chatted, he began to recount a story he had heard a pastor tell the previous Sunday, a lesson learned from a "personal evangelistic encounter." I found myself getting angry as he talked, but I tried to keep my face from revealing how I felt.

I'll tell you up front that I was upset for two reasons. First, I knew the story was not true. It was one of those Christian "urban legends" I had heard many times through the years (stories that are commonly told but aren't actually true), but the pastor had presented this story as if it were his own experience. Second, the tale told by the pastor was based on some bad theology and was intended to foist tremendous guilt on the listener.

Here's the story—you've probably heard a version of it before.

"I was talking with my friend, Dan, about Jesus. I shared about God's grace and the need for all people to receive Jesus as the one who can forgive their sins and be Lord of their lives. I walked Dan through the gospel, but I didn't force the point of decision. I failed to call him to respond right then and there.

"After our conversation, Dan walked out of the building and into the street and was hit by a truck. He died right there on the spot. Now I have to live the rest of my life, and all of eternity, knowing that Dan could have been in heaven if I had been bold enough to push the issue and if I had called him to a point of commitment."

This story and others like it end up heaping pressure, guilt, and fear on believers in a poor attempt to motivate them to do outreach. It communicates to the listener that if we don't do our part just right, people will end up in hell—and it will be all our fault! This line of thinking places a great burden of responsibility on us, way more than the Bible calls us to bear. Remember, we scatter seed and water it, but only God changes lives. If someone refuses the grace offered in Jesus, we do not live with the blame in this life or eternity.

Our Partnership with the Spirit

As we collaborate with God to reach out to others, we must understand that only the Spirit of God can convict a person of sin. We can share our story of being saved from our sins. We can even explain to a nonbeliever what the Bible teaches about sin and the need for a Savior. But only God's Spirit can convict sinners of their need for the grace of Jesus. In the gospel of John, Jesus teaches about the coming of the Holy Spirit and the work that he will do: "When he comes, he will convict the world of guilt in regard to sin and righteousness and judgment" (John 16:8). We partner with the Spirit with great faith, knowing that God will do what he has promised to do—bring conviction of sin.

The Spirit's Answers to Our "What Ifs"

The book of Acts teaches us many lessons about how the Holy Spirit is alive and active in the process of outreach. When we feel inadequate for the task of evangelism, the truth revealed in the history of the early church can fortify and encourage us. Following are some common questions we may wrestle with as we partner with God in the work of outreach.

WHAT IF I LACK THE POWER TO REACH OUT EFFECTIVELY?

The Bible presupposes that we *lack* the strength, power, and boldness to reach out effectively. You are not alone if you feel you lack the energy or boldness to share your faith. In fact, you are in good company. Jesus told his disciples, "You will receive *power* when the Holy Spirit comes on you; and you will be my witnesses in Jerusalem, and in all Judea and Samaria, and to the ends of the earth" (Acts 1:8, emphasis added).

Peter is a perfect example of this reality. He was so fearful of the religious leaders that he denied Jesus three times (Matt. 26:69–75).

Then at Pentecost, as the Spirit came on him, Peter preached with a level of clarity and conviction that was clearly Spirit-anointed (Acts 2). What changed Peter from a fearful denier into a bold proclaimer? Later in Acts we see the answer: "Then Peter, filled with the Holy Spirit, said to them: 'Rulers and elders of the people! If we are being called to account today for an act of kindness shown to a cripple and are asked how he was healed, then know this, you and all the people of Israel: It is by the name of Jesus Christ of Nazareth, whom you crucified but whom God raised from the dead, that this man stands before you healed'" (Acts 4:8–10). In a matter of moments Peter accused the religious leaders of killing the Messiah and boldly declared that "salvation is found in no one else, for there is no other name under heaven given to men by which we must be saved" (Acts 4:12). These are gutsy words from a guy who avoided confrontation with these same leaders just days earlier.

The difference between the two Peters? The Holy Spirit.

In the New Testament, when the Spirit came in power, the gospel was shared and lives were changed (Acts 2:1–38; 10:44–48; 11:15–17). The early followers of Jesus were an important part of God's plan to bring the message of Jesus to the world, but without the work of the Spirit, their efforts would have been futile.

Our calling is not to muster up some sort of inner courage so we can reach out with God's love. We find our strength and passion as we tune in to the presence and voice of the Holy Spirit. If you feel as if your power will not be enough to get the job of outreach done, ask for God's Spirit to infuse you with strength and surprise you with boldness. You'll be amazed what God will do in and through you by his Holy Spirit.

What If I Don't Know What to Do Next?

The book of Acts also gives hope to those of us who wonder how we will know what to do, where to go, and what to say as we seek to reach out in Jesus' name. Again, reliance on the Holy Spirit is essential.

The apostle Paul was told where to go by the leading of the Holy Spirit. "During the night Paul had a vision of a man of Macedonia standing and begging him, 'Come over to Macedonia and help us.'

After Paul had seen the vision, we got ready at once to leave for Macedonia, concluding that God had called us to preach the gospel to them" (Acts 16:9–10). Interestingly, right before this vision, the Spirit had directed Paul to avoid certain places. "Paul and his companions traveled throughout the region of Phrygia and Galatia, having been kept by the Holy Spirit from preaching the word in the province of Asia. When they came to the border of Mysia, they tried to enter Bithynia, but the Spirit of Jesus would not allow them to" (Acts 16:6–7).

This kind of direction was not reserved for Paul alone. It was normative for all of God's servants. Phillip was directed to a specific place where God orchestrated a divine encounter with an Ethiopian who was desperately seeking the truth (Acts 8:26–40). Before this meeting was over, the man had received Jesus and been baptized. Peter also received divine direction as he engaged in evangelism. The Holy Spirit spoke to both him and Cornelius, a spiritual seeker (Acts 10). The hand of God was all over that encounter, and it led to a powerful manifestation of the Spirit, a baptism, and the transformation of a whole family! If we also keep in mind Jesus' promise that his sheep will hear and recognize his voice (John 10:4), we can be confident that God is ready to guide us as we reach out to others. We don't have to figure it all out on our own.

I was reminded of this truth when I was getting ready for a trip to the West Coast. I knew I was going to have the chance to see one specific family member who had not yet responded to the gospel. I spent a great deal of time praying for an opportunity to share Christ with this person. As I prayed, I felt the Holy Spirit fill me with hope and even begin to form words and thoughts to share during my upcoming visit. God was on the move!

A few days before I traveled, I got a call from another family member who lovingly warned me that this might not be a good time to enter into spiritual conversations with the person I had been praying for.

I faced quite a dilemma. I had clearly felt the Holy Spirit inspiring me and giving me words to say. I knew God had been directing my prayers and preparing my heart. And so I had to decide if I would follow the leading of the Spirit or heed the words of a family member I respected and loved. The answer was difficult but also quite obvious—follow God! By God's grace, I shared my thoughts with this family member during my visit, and this trip became a pivotal moment in her spiritual journey—she prayed to receive Jesus!

As followers of Christ, we don't have to manipulate situations or force decisions. Instead, we should listen for the whisper of the Spirit. When the Spirit says, "Go," we get moving. If he says, "Not that way," we hit the brakes. If we want to be effective in reaching out with the love and message of Jesus, we will listen for the Holy Spirit's voice and follow his lead.

WHAT IF I COME UNDER THE ENEMY'S ATTACK?

If we partner with the Spirit of God in sharing the good news of Jesus, the question is not, "Will I come under attack?" Rather, the question is, "When will the enemy mount his next assault?" Since our battle is not against flesh and blood (Eph. 6:12), we know the enemy won't sit idly by while we reach out with the message and love of Jesus. We face an ongoing battle in this world and need the presence and power of the Holy Spirit to carry us through.

Once when the apostle Paul had a chance to witness to a man who needed Jesus, a sorcerer came against Paul:

> But Elymas the sorcerer (for that is what his name means) opposed them and tried to turn the proconsul from the faith. Then Saul, who was also called Paul, filled with the Holy Spirit, looked straight at Elymas and said, "You are a child of the devil and an enemy of everything that is right! You are full of all kinds of deceit and trickery. Will you never stop perverting the right ways of the Lord? Now the hand of the Lord is against you. You are going to be blind, and for a time you will be unable to see the light of the sun."
>
> Immediately mist and darkness came over him, and he groped about, seeking someone to lead him by the hand. When the proconsul saw what had happened, he believed, for he was amazed at the teaching about the Lord.
>
> —Acts 13:8–12

Paul didn't have the power to overcome this spiritual attack of the enemy, but the Holy Spirit was more than strong enough.

As Jesus walked this earth and brought his kingdom into human history, he faced a constant battle against demonic powers. As his ambassadors on the earth today, we too will face this battle. The key is to allow the Spirit in us to do the fighting. In 1 John we read, "You, dear children, are from God and have overcome them, because the one who is in you is greater than the one who is in the world" (4:4). The Spirit who dwells in each and every believer has power over any work of the enemy. In James we read, "Submit yourselves, then, to God. Resist the devil, and he will flee from you. Come near to God and he will come near to you" (4:7–8). As we draw near to God, resist the enemy, and embrace the astounding power of Jesus, the enemy runs.

As evangelism becomes an organic part of your daily life, don't be surprised when the enemy tries to trip you up and stop your outreach efforts. Learn to recognize his attacks, cry out for the power of the Spirit to overcome the enemy, and draw near to God. Know that the Holy Spirit who dwells in you, through faith in Jesus, is infinitely more powerful than the devil and his minions. Stand in the power of the Spirit and press forward with the gospel.

We are a big part of God's plan for bringing the good news of Jesus to our generation. We are given the privilege and the responsibility of teaming up with God to bring his grace and truth to the world. But we must never forget that in this partnership, the Holy Spirit is always the senior partner. We don't get credit when someone comes to faith in Jesus—we get to celebrate! In the same way, though, we don't bear the blame if someone chooses to reject the gospel. The work of evangelism can feel lonely, but we are never truly alone. The Spirit of God goes before us to prepare our path, walks beside us to give guidance, and follows behind us to offer protection every step of the way.

BEARING KINGDOM FRUIT

Organic Activity: I Can Do That!

- *What's Next?* The Spirit of God will close and open doors so you can stay on track with his plans to reach your family and friends. Take time to surrender your daily schedule and plans to the leading of the Spirit. Ask God to give you eyes to see and ears to hear; let him know that if he gives a specific direction or opens a door, you are ready to follow. Also, if God has opened a door but you have been fearful about walking through it, commit to take that step as soon as possible.

- *Go to Battle.* Identify where the enemy is on the attack against your outreach efforts or against someone you are trying to reach with the gospel. Commit to partner with the Holy Spirit as you pray and stand against this point of attack. You might want to meditate on Ephesians 6:10–18 as you pray for power to resist the devil. As he flees, thank God and press forward with the next step in your calling to reach out.

Personal Reflection

- Are there ways I subtly seek to take credit for the work God does in reaching people and changing lives? If so, how can I be more intentional about giving God the glory and not taking it for myself?

- Are there ways I take too much responsibility for people's response to Jesus? If I am living with a sense of blame because some people have not come to faith, how can I release this feeling and gain a more balanced perspective on my part in the work of outreach?

- How have I seen the Holy Spirit move hearts and touch lives? As I reflect on the work of the Spirit in the past, how might I be inspired to trust in the Spirit's work in the future?

Group Reflection

- Read the quote by Bill Hybels on the first page of this chapter. Why is being "cooperative with the Holy Spirit" so critical when it comes to our outreach efforts? What does it mean to have "an ear fine-tuned to the promptings of the Holy Spirit"?
- Henry's story is a reminder that the Holy Spirit is at work in the conversion process. Tell about a time you saw the Spirit intervene and do something no person could have done in the process of leading someone to Jesus.
- What are the potential dangers of taking the credit when a person comes to faith in Jesus? What are the potential dangers of taking the blame if a person does not respond to the gospel and receive Jesus?

Prayer Direction

Spirit of God, thank you for inviting me to be a partner with you in the glorious ministry of reaching people whose hearts are far from the Father. Help me see you at work with sharper vision. Open my ears to hear your voice speaking at a higher volume. Move in me and through me with such power that I feel your boldness flowing freely. And where the enemy rears his ugly head and tries to keep people in his clutches and under the tyranny of his influence, work through me, in Jesus' name, and set captives free. Amen.

Chapter 11

Engaging in Spiritual CONVERSATIONS

Spiritual conversations don't have to be forced and uncomfortable. They can be a natural part of our lives. God wants our faith to overflow into our daily interactions in organic ways. If our faith is real, it will be part of our ordinary conversations.

But in your hearts set apart Christ as Lord. Always be pre-
pared to give an answer to everyone who asks you to give the
reason for the hope that you have. But do this with gentleness
and respect.

—1 Peter 3:15

Then they called them in again and commanded them not to
speak or teach at all in the name of Jesus. But Peter and John
replied, "Judge for yourselves whether it is right in God's sight
to obey you rather than God. For we cannot help speaking
about what we have seen and heard."

—Acts 4:18–20

God has put a message within you. When you become a be-
liever, you also become God's messenger. God wants to speak
to the world through you. Paul said, "We speak the truth be-
fore God, as messengers of God" (2 Corinthians 2:1, NCV).
You have a storehouse of experiences that God wants to use to
bring others into his family.

—Rick Warren, in
The Complete
Evangelism Handbook

Several years ago, while traveling on a plane from Chicago to London, I experienced one of the most profound moments in all my years of following Jesus. The weather was severe, we had been delayed a number of times already, and I had been moved to a different plane, losing my reserved seat. When I finally found my spot on the plane, it was neither an aisle nor a window seat. I just wanted to buckle my seat belt, put on my headphones, and go to sleep!

But God had something else in mind. I was about to learn that almost anyone I meet might be open to a spiritual conversation. And even though I tell the full story in my book *Seismic Shifts*, a portion of it bears retelling here.

Often when I get on a plane, I look forward to meeting people, chatting, and even praying for a natural opportunity to talk about my relationship with Jesus. This was not one of those times.

A young German woman in her early twenties ended up sitting next to me. She was warm, friendly, and looking for a conversation. Her name was Gretchen, and I think it would be fair to say that she was probably the last person I expected to have a spiritual conversation with. Gretchen was an atheist, a humanist, *and* a communist. She even worked at a camp that taught high-school-age students to maintain their atheistic worldview amid the incoming flood of Christianity into the former East Germany.

I asked her about the core beliefs she held as an atheist and a humanist. I listened to her for over an hour. She spoke passionately about her love for the young people of her nation and her deep concern that they not be corrupted by the hate-mongering and small-mindedness of Christianity. I have to say, even though I disagreed with her, I liked her honesty and passion.

After more than an hour of telling me about her world, her dreams, and her passions, Gretchen turned to me and asked, "So what do you do?"

I responded with a lighthearted chuckle, "Kind of the same as you—except the exact opposite!"

Her eyes got real big and she stared at me, waiting for an explanation.

"This might come as a surprise, but I'm a Christian! Actually, I'm a Christian pastor."

She looked both puzzled and skeptical.

I continued, "I spend my life trying to help people learn about the love of God and the great news of Jesus Christ. I guess I'm one of those people you are trying to keep away from the youth of your country."

An awkward silence hung in the air. I wasn't sure how she would respond to my revelation. But to my surprise, Gretchen thanked me. She thanked me for listening to her story and not condemning her. She told me that she had never had a conversation with a Christian that lasted more than five minutes. She said that most of the time, once a Christian finds out what she believes, the conversation ends abruptly. She thanked me for being interested in her life and beliefs.

I asked Gretchen if she would like to hear my story and learn about my philosophical worldview. She said yes with no small measure of excitement, so I spent the next hour telling her about how I had come from a nonbelieving family with a mother who was a math and science teacher and a father who was a computer programmer. I told her about my journey from the borderlands of unbelief into the arms of a loving God. I explained how Jesus had become my best friend when I embraced faith in his life, death, and resurrection as historical realities. I even took a risk and shared with her that I believe all my sins are washed away because of what Jesus did on the cross. I explained, as best I could, how the community of believers I am a part of is filled with loving and warm people whom I thought she would really enjoy meeting. I even pointed out that many of her beliefs as a humanistic communist reflected that her heart wasn't far from the heart of God. Earlier in our conversation, Gretchen had said, "I am a humanist because I believe there is value and dignity in every human life. Everyone matters!" I told her that this is Jesus' message and that it is why he came to this earth. She was fascinated.

After more than two hours of conversing, she agreed that we were much closer to each other than she had ever dreamed. I encouraged her to investigate the message of Jesus and see if her heart might be drawn to him. I also invited her to pray and ask God, "If you are really out there, reveal yourself to me." She seemed intrigued by the thought of praying to a God she did not believe in.

Since that day I have lived with a firm conviction that almost anyone is open to entering into a spiritual conversation, if we speak with gentleness and respect. If a communistic, humanistic atheist who worked at a camp to protect young people from Christians was open to having a spiritual conversation, hearing my story of faith, and listening to a simple presentation of the gospel, I have to believe almost anyone is open.

Engaging in Organic Conversations

There are all kinds of spiritual conversations we can enter into. Some might be brief chats about the beauty of creation. Or we might talk about the gift of family life and the people we love, giving thanks to God for his blessings. Other times we might share a story of how God is working in our lives and moving in real ways. As the Holy Spirit opens doors, we will encounter times when sharing our conversion story is entirely appropriate and natural. We need to learn how to identify what kind of conversation is appropriate in each of life's varied settings.

It is unhealthy and inauthentic to try to unload a memorized script on people. Instead, our faith and love for Jesus should flow naturally into our daily conversations. By the Holy Spirit's leading, we can assess each situation and discover a person's level of interest and openness. One nonbelieving friend might be highly responsive, while another could be defensive and closed off to spiritual things. Until we identify where a person is in their spiritual journey, it will be difficult to have a good conversation.

Many Levels of Conversation

In their book *What's Gone Wrong with the Harvest*, James Engel and Wilbert Norton propose a whole spectrum of spiritual conversations we can have with people who are not yet followers of Jesus.[35] So often we think of spiritual conversations in the narrow sense of sharing our testimony and presenting the gospel. But there are really many different ways we can enter into meaningful, spiritual conversations with people.

Engel and Norton expand our understanding of where non-Christians are coming from by using a simple scale.[36] The scale ranges from minus eight (representing someone with no knowledge of the gospel) to zero (representing the point of conversion) to positive five (reflecting a Christian who is mature in faith). Their insights helped open my mind to the reality that spiritual conversations can and should take place at every point on the continuum.

Such a scale might feel contrived to some. I certainly don't advocate using specific numbers to categorize people or lock them into a man-made group. But I do find the scale concept to be a helpful reminder that spiritually disconnected people can be found everywhere we look, and each is at a different place in their relationship with God. Recognizing this will make us more sensitive when we talk with them about issues of faith.

For example, if a believer is interacting with someone at negative seven on the scale, a brief chat about the beauty of creation and the thought that there might be a loving and creative God behind the glory of a sunset might help nudge them closer to the Savior. This conversation represents forward movement—a cause for celebration! In a similar way, someone at negative one might be ready for a conversation in which the gospel is laid out with clarity and conviction. Followers of Christ need to be ready to have meaningful conversations with people along a broad continuum.

Thom Rainer, in his book *The Unchurched Next Door*, raises a similar insight, suggesting that nonbelievers are on a continuum of openness.[37] Rainer uses the image of a door and asks us to consider the various states of the door between fully open and fully closed. He then uses the letter *U* to represent various types of unchurched people. In Thom's words, a U5 person is "highly antagonistic and even hostile to the gospel." For this person, the door is fully closed. A U4 person is "resistant to the gospel" but does not have an antagonistic attitude; the door is open, but merely a crack. A U3 person is in a "neutral place." This person may not show signs of being interested but is open to discussion; the door is open a bit more. A U2 person is "receptive, interested and curious" about the gospel; the door is almost all the way open. Finally, a U1 person is "highly receptive" to hearing and receiving the good news; the door is flung wide open.[38]

Rainer interviews unchurched and unbelieving people to learn from them. From his conversations, he has learned that people are in all kinds of different places. We Christians tend to be a bit simplistic in our thinking and often lump all unbelievers in one group. I believe this is a mistake. The way we relate to unbelievers should be shaped by an awareness of where they are in relationship to God. How open is the door of their heart?

The insights of Thom Rainer and the team of Engel and Norton only begin to awaken us to the beautiful complexity of carrying on spiritual conversations. We can't rely on rote responses to every question. Spiritual conversation should be seen as an art form, not a science project.

Sharing Our Pain and Brokenness

Sometimes Christians feel as if they should have it all together. We think that people expect us to be perfect. But the reality is that we are all broken vessels and are gradually being pieced back together by the grace of Jesus. We don't have all the answers to life, but we know Jesus, and we know that he is the answer to our greatest need. Our lives are not perfect, but we do experience a very real joy that only God can bring, even in the hardest of times.

A dear friend named Karen shared a story that vividly brought this truth to life for me. Karen goes to a woman named Cindy to have her nails done. She had been praying for God to open the door for spiritual conversations, but Cindy had been fairly resistant, tending to shut down when spiritual topics came up.

One day Karen was heading in to have her nails done but was unsure whether she should even go. Her daughter had battled a life-threatening illness for over two decades, and she had just received some difficult news from the doctors. Since she was feeling weak and discouraged, Karen didn't want to show her true self to Cindy. She was afraid that Cindy would see her weakness and be turned off to the Christian faith. Despite her concern, Karen decided she could put on a bold outer appearance and make it through the appointment without breaking down.

But when Karen sat down to have her nails done, Cindy innocently asked, "How are you doing?" And that was all it took—the floodgates broke and Karen's pain and struggle came pouring out. She wept and ended up telling Cindy all about her journey with her daughter, whom she loved so much. But here's the amazing thing. As Karen told her story, her faith came through organically! She talked about how she never could have made it through all the years and all the tests and uncertainty without Jesus walking at her side and holding her hand each step of the way.

Karen and Cindy's friendship moved to a whole new level as Cindy was able to care for Karen. It also deepened because the two women were able to have a significant spiritual conversation that included the topics of pain, struggle, God's sustaining power, and the grace of Jesus in hard times.

Karen didn't plot out the conversation; it came naturally as she was real about her struggles and her faith in Christ. At some point in her life, Karen had bought into the lie that she always had to appear as though she had it all together. The reality is that spiritual seekers will never listen to us if we put on a facade and present ourselves as perfect people, untouched by the pain and brokenness in this world. Sharing our struggles honestly and helping people see how God is with us in the hard times can lead to some wonderful spiritual conversations. Our friends and family members who are not followers of Jesus will begin to wonder if there might be a God out there who could help them through the storms of their lives. Sharing our pains and struggles gives us a chance to witness to the God who promises to be a shelter, a stronghold, and a mighty tower of protection in the storms of life.

Sharing Uncertainty

Even as we are honest about our pain and brokenness, we should be equally willing to admit that we don't have all the answers to life's questions. Christians aren't always certain about everything in this life, in our faith, or even in the Bible. In chapter 3 I discussed the importance of having a humble confidence in the Bible, but this confidence is very different from declaring that we understand everything with absolute clarity. God is just way too big for us to proudly declare that we have every aspect of our lives and faith nailed down. The fact that we still struggle with our own questions will help unbelievers see that they don't need to have everything figured out before surrendering their lives to Jesus.

A clear biblical example of this concept is the blind man in John 9. This man had come to faith in Jesus through a powerful healing encounter. Now the religious authorities were asking him complex questions that he was not equipped to answer. Instead of pretending he had it all figured out, the man *admitted what he did not know* and *affirmed what he did know.* He said of Jesus, "Whether he is a sinner or not, I don't know. One thing I do know. I was blind but now I see!" (John 9:25). When we are honest about our uncertainties, we can also be bold about what we know with confidence.

When I encounter a person who struggles with why there is so much pain in the world, I have to be honest and admit that I wonder about this too. They might even say, "How can a loving God allow so much violence and suffering?" I don't try to give a tight defense of God and tell them it's easy to understand why suffering exists. Instead, I enter into an honest conversation and struggle with them.

I am not ashamed to admit that I have a hard time understanding why thousands of women are sold into sex slavery every year, why entire towns can be buried under the rubble of an earthquake, or why AIDS is devastating entire countries in Africa. In these moments, I don't try to defend God; I just listen and share my own struggles over the violence and pain that so many experience.

As the conversation presses on, I might recommend they read the first chapter of Lee Strobel's book *The Case for Faith.*[39] Strobel does a better job than I could ever do of walking through biblical and logical arguments for how suffering can exist in a universe created and sustained by a loving God. We may be able to provide reasonable answers to many of the questions that spiritual seekers raise, but sometimes the best response is to be honest and say, "That's a great question, and I wonder about that sometimes too."

When I run into people who are wondering about all the different world religions and how anyone can be sure that their faith is trustworthy and true, I don't give the glib answer, "I just know they are all wrong and my faith is right!" Instead, I ask questions about their faith background and talk about what my faith means to me. I do my best to explain the solid historical evidence that supports the Christian faith. Often I direct them to a great book like *Choosing Your Faith* by Mark Mittelberg.[40] In this resource they will get far more help than I can offer.

When people question the Bible or mention things they just don't understand, I usually say something like, "Join the club! I'm still trying to figure out lots of things—and I'm a pastor!" I don't question the authority or truth of God's Word; I believe that every single word of the Bible is breathed by God (2 Tim. 3:16) and that the Scriptures are true from the first word of Genesis to the last word of Revelation. But I do confess that there are things in the Bible I don't fully understand. God is bigger than me, and his ways are higher than mine. I'm comfortable admitting that I don't have everything in the Bible figured out.

Admitting we don't have all the answers will often open the door for ongoing conversation. Jack Strack, in *The Complete Evangelism Guidebook*, writes, "When I'm faced with a question that I'm unable to answer completely, I admit that I don't have all the information, but because I care about the person asking the question, I will go to others or spend more time in study to get a more complete answer."[41] When we are in a spiritual conversation and someone asks a question we can't answer, it is usually wise just to say, "Let me do a little study or reflect on that and get back to you." Some Christians feel like they need to have all the answers, so they make up an answer on the spot. This is unwise. Instead, just humbly admit, "That's a great question, and I don't have a good answer right now. Let me get back to you on that." Then make sure to follow up with the person and share what you have learned.

Great Questions to Ask

As you watch for the Holy Spirit to open doors for spiritual conversations, you can ask some questions that might spark meaningful interaction. Don't be afraid to ask good questions and really listen to people's answers. The point of a well-asked question is not to set you up to unload your spiritual wisdom on others, but to create space for meaningful discussion. Of course, if the door opens to share your story of faith or the gospel message, then wonderful! Walk through that door. But you can have a meaningful spiritual conversation without having to close it with a gospel presentation.

Here are some questions that could move your conversations with nonbelievers to deeper levels of spiritual interaction:

- *What are some joys you are experiencing in this season of your life?* Most people would love to share about the good things in their lives, but they are afraid that others won't care. Just by asking and listening, you open the door for great interaction. Also, if there are clear signs that God is blessing their life, you could open the door for conversation about the source of all good things.

- *What challenges and struggles are you facing?* People will share their pains and hurts with someone who truly cares about them and takes the time to listen. As they share, you may find that it becomes an opportunity to minister the grace of Jesus. Sharing struggles can also create space for you to pray *for* or *with* them. (See chapters 6 and 7 in this book.)

- *What is your personal history when it comes to faith and God?* This question is not so much about what people believe as it is about their personal histories. A person might say, "I have no history when it comes to religion," or "I grew up going to Mass every week and my parents are quite devout," or "I have always been very spiritual and I still read my horoscope daily and do a lot of meditation." No matter what answer they give, you end up learning something about their journey that may allow you to move the conversation to a deeper level.

- *What do you believe about God?* With this question, we move into more personal convictions and beliefs. Again, no matter how they answer, remember that you are learning and already going deeper than a typical conversation. Some Christians feel pressured to correct "wrong thinking" or "errant theology" in their conversations with nonbelievers. Try not to do this. Just listen and learn where they are; then you'll gain a sense of where they still need to go on their journey toward Jesus.

• *What is your perception of Christians?* Or put a different way, "What is your perception of Christianity or of the Christian church?" It takes courage to ask this question, listen, and not get defensive. But I have found that it can be an open door to deeper conversations.

When it comes to asking good questions, the key is to keep them open-ended. Create space to talk. Don't become defensive and tell people where they are wrong. Just listen, learn, hear their hearts, and get a sense of where they are in their spiritual journeys. Even an angry atheist is on a journey. They are just very far from God. By listening to their perspective, you can learn how to pray, reach out, and walk with them toward the Savior.

Truck-Sized Openings

Some situations naturally create open doors for spiritual conversations. I call these "openings you could drive a truck through." These times almost beg for believers to share something about their relationship with God. Here are a few examples:

• *When someone asks you, "Hey, what did you do this weekend?"* It doesn't matter if you're a high school student, an at-home-parent, an office worker, or a retired person—there's a good chance that every Monday someone will ask you this divinely appointed question: "What did you do this weekend?" If you gathered with God's people for worship, make sure you talk about it. Give an honest answer. "Well, I worked in my yard, watched some football, and had an amazing time at church. My pastor talked about how to manage your finances in a tough economy and how to discover what is worth investing in. What he shared was practical and very helpful. Oh, and I watched some NASCAR on Sunday afternoon." By talking about being part of a church and learning helpful things in worship, you let your faith shine through. Your friend might even ask what you learned about finances. You could get a CD of the message if they are interested, or you could direct them to your church website (if your church offers free downloads of messages). Each weekend when you go to church, identify one part of the message or service that was powerful and practical. Be ready to tell others about it when they ask about your weekend.

- *When you are talking with a friend and sharing a struggle or hurt in your life.* Be sure to talk honestly about the difficulty of walking through this season of life, but also give testimony to how God has shown up, sustained you, and helped you through. Spiritual seekers want to know if our faith is real; they want to know if it makes a difference in daily life.

- *When you are experiencing a time of blessing, joy, or celebration.* There are times in life when it is appropriate to acknowledge that the good things you are experiencing come from the hand of a loving God. When others notice you are in a good place and see that you are filled with joy, don't hesitate to let them know that your faith in God plays a key part in this.

- *When you are viewing the power and beauty of creation.* A lightning storm, a calm day on the lake, the crashing of ocean waves, a star-pierced sky, and a fresh blanket of snow on the ground all tell of God's creative power. When you experience these moments with a friend or family member who is not a Christian, don't be shy about acknowledging the one who made the heavens and the earth and everything in them. Don't let this turn into a debate with them, but simply keep it a personal acknowledgment that God is the most amazing artist in the universe.

You'll have other opportune moments in everyday conversation for the discussion of faith, but take advantage of these recurring moments in life that can lead to natural and rich spiritual conversations.

Because God is Lord over the entire universe, every moment in life has a spiritual dynamic. Nothing falls outside his gaze or extends beyond his interest. Every conversation we have with another person has some relation to God and the spiritual realities of life.

The key to engaging in effective spiritual conversations is to find ways for them to be an organic part of life. Pray that God will enter into the flow of your day. Since your faith is real and Jesus is engrafted into every area of your life, spiritual topics should come up naturally throughout your day. Remember that you are not forcing your faith onto others; rather, it is part of your heart and life and is entirely appropriate for it to come up in daily conversation.

BEARING KINGDOM FRUIT

Organic Activity: I Can Do That!

- *Prepare to Share.* This chapter includes four examples of natural moments that open the door for deeper spiritual conversations. One of them is how you respond to the question, "What did you do this weekend?" This week, when you gather for worship with God's people, identify one or more elements of the worship experience that you might share with a nonbelieving friend. Then when you talk about your weekend, make sure you tell your friend about an encounter with God in worship, a lesson learned from the sermon, or a connection you made with one of God's people. Don't memorize a speech, but prepare to share some part of your spiritual journey from the weekend.
- *Ask Questions.* Identify one of the five questions offered in this chapter that might spark a spiritual conversation with a non-Christian friend. Pray for an opportunity to ask one of these questions and take time to really listen. You'll be amazed at the doors God can open through a good question and an honest conversation.

Personal Reflection

- Using one of the scales discussed in this chapter (Engel and Norton's or Thom Rainer's), where would I place one or two of my nonbelieving friends? In light of their openness, or lack of openness, what level of spiritual conversation would be appropriate with each person?

How might I help nudge the conversation to a new level of spiritual engagement?

- What pain and struggles have I faced in my life, and how has God been near me through these hard times? What might happen if I shared these experiences honestly with a nonbelieving friend? How might my story of God's comforting presence and sustaining power bring hope to others?

Group Reflection

- What helps you enter naturally into spiritual conversations with family members and friends who are not yet followers of Jesus?
- Tell about a time when God surprised you by opening the door for a spiritual conversation.
- This chapter includes a warning to be careful about memorizing a spiritual speech and unleashing it on people. What are the dangers of presenting a memorized script? What is the value of learning good conversation starters and then letting the Spirit direct where things go?
- Do you agree that you should be willing to admit that you don't have all the answers and still struggle with some of your own questions when it comes to faith and the Bible? Why or why not?

Prayer Direction

Jesus, you are the living Word of God. You have given us the Bible so we have your written Word. Please help me when I speak with my nonbelieving friends. Give me the right words. Sometimes I don't know what to say, and other times I get nervous that I will say the wrong thing. But I want to talk freely about you, my faith, and all you mean to me. I want others to know you are real. Help me to love you so deeply that your goodness comes up naturally in my conversations. By your Holy Spirit, anoint my lips so I can have many conversations that will help people see you more clearly and want to know you personally. Amen.

CHAPTER 12

Telling Your STORY

Christians don't have just one testimony; we have many. Our testimonies are stories of God's power and presence in our lives. Every new day brings fresh stories of God's goodness and grace.

Then, leaving her water jar, the woman went back to the town and said to the people, "Come, see a man who told me everything I ever did. Could this be the Christ?"

—John 4:28–29

Then Paul said: "I am a Jew, born in Tarsus of Cilicia, but brought up in this city. Under Gamaliel I was thoroughly trained in the law of our fathers and was just as zealous for God as any of you are today. I persecuted the followers of this Way to their death, arresting both men and women and throwing them into prison, as also the high priest and all the Council can testify. I even obtained letters from them to their brothers in Damascus, and went there to bring these people as prisoners to Jerusalem to be punished.
"About noon as I came near Damascus, suddenly a bright light from heaven flashed around me. I fell to the ground and heard a voice say to me, 'Saul! Saul! Why do you persecute me?'
" 'Who are you, Lord?' I asked.
" 'I am Jesus of Nazareth, whom you are persecuting,' he replied."

—Acts 22:3–8

Every Christian has a personal story to tell.... God has called you to be a very specific, very special person, and your story, your life, is a testimony to God's goodness, his grace, his forgiveness. So share who you are with people. Let them know you have struggles, but that God has made a difference.

—Rebecca M. Pippert,
Out of the Saltshaker

Story 1: A Changed Relationship

For a good portion of my life, I didn't care very much about people. I spent most of my time doing what would make me happy. If that meant stepping on those around me, so be it! One person who got caught in the collateral damage of my self-centered life was my sister. She was kind to me, but I treated her poorly. I didn't even realize how unkind I was being toward a member of my own family.

Then I began to learn about Jesus and his love for me. My sister was actually the one who dared to tell me about God's care and why Jesus came to this earth. Over time, I came to understand—I got it! I came to believe that Jesus is exactly who he said he is, and I asked him to take away all the wrongs I had done and to lead my life. Not only did Jesus forgive me, but he also began teaching me how to love others. Things began to change in my life.

For the first time in my life, I went out of my way to do something kind for my sister. She was quite busy at the time, so I tried to help her by doing some work around the house that she was responsible for. She was shocked and wondered if it was some kind of trick instead of an act of kindness. With my record of cruelty, I can't blame her for being suspicious. She looked at me and said, "Why did you do that?" I locked eyes with her and said, with all sincerity, "Because I love you." That moment marked the beginning of a friendship that continues growing to this day. Only God could change a heart like mine.

Story 2: New Purpose

I had no purpose for living. I had no motivation to work hard at anything. I was becoming a bum, just doing what I had to do to get by. The idea of ever getting married, having a kid, working a real job, or doing anything that demanded some effort was a foreign concept to me. I saw nothing on the horizon to change my outlook on life.

Live ... die ... end of story.

At a point when I had become fatalistic and discouraged with life, I met Jesus Christ. He gave me a reason to live. He showed me that my life matters. When I surrendered my heart to him and received his forgiveness for all my wrongs, something in me was changed. His friendship and love gave me a new vision.

I can honestly say that I live each day with a deep sense of purpose and meaning. God has put me on this earth to love him and the people around me. I have a wonderful wife and a beautiful family, I love the work I do, and every day is a new adventure of walking with Jesus.

Story 3: From Fear to Faith

Fear was part of the landscape of my life. Since I had no belief system and no faith in God, the idea of death hung over me like a dark cloud. I had watched people I loved pass away, and I had no category for these moments of life. What was on the other side? Was there more to life than seventy years and a coffin? I had no answers to these big questions.

Out of the blue I was invited to some church activities and started to learn that the Bible has answers to some of the big questions that had lurked in the corners of my mind. I found out that Jesus died on the cross to wash away all our wrongs and then came back to life again. He took on death, a one-on-one battle, and he scored a definitive win! Not only did he die and then rise from the dead, but he offers new life now and for eternity to everyone who believes in him. I asked for his victory to be mine and became part of his family.

I don't live with fear anymore. I know Jesus is in me and will lead me every day of this life. Then when this life ends, I will go to be with him forever. This life is just the warm-up band; the big show is still to come.

Followers of Jesus don't have one testimony; we have many. Because God is active and working in our lives, we have new stories to tell every day. These stories, or testimonies, recount how God is present and powerful. The three stories that open this chapter are all testimonies of the same person—me. I could write another fifty pages of testimony after testimony of how God has moved, worked, and transformed my life.

Not a Testimony, but Testimonies

As we walk with spiritually disconnected people, we are always praying for an opportunity to tell "God's story," the gospel. At the same time, we also will have opportunities to tell *our stories* about the difference God has made, and is making, in our lives. A testimony is the telling of our story in an authentic and compelling way. In John 4 we read about a woman telling the story of her encounter with Jesus:

> Then, leaving her water jar, the woman went back to the town and said to the people, "Come, see a man who told me everything I ever did. Could this be the Christ?" They came out of the town and made their way toward him....
>
> Many of the Samaritans from that town believed in him because of the woman's testimony, "He told me everything I ever did." So when the Samaritans came to him, they urged him to stay with them, and he stayed two days. And because of his words many more became believers.
>
> They said to the woman, "We no longer believe just because of what you said; now we have heard for ourselves, and we know that this man really is the Savior of the world."
>
> —vv. 28–30; 39–42

This woman met Jesus and had a spiritual conversation with him, and the eyes of her heart were opened. She came to embrace him as the long-awaited Messiah. She was changed!

What did she do next? She hurried to town and told others what had happened in her heart. This woman had been in the habit of avoiding the townspeople; she'd even been going to the well in the heat of the day to avoid the other women who came in the cool of the morning. But now she had a story to tell, a personal testimony about the power of Jesus to change a life—her life. Many people from the town ended up believing in Jesus because of her testimony.

For a long time Christians have thought of a personal testimony as a memorized speech that tells how they became a follower of Jesus. While telling about what happened in your life when you first followed Jesus can be valuable, most disconnected people are more interested in what Jesus is doing in your life today. They want to know if there really is something to this Christian faith. If there is a God, does he have the power to help them experience true and lasting transformation?

An authentic witness to what God has done in our lives speaks volumes. As I've noted elsewhere, *many people outside the church do not believe that we believe what we say we believe.* Let that truth sink in, and make it personal. *Many spiritually disconnected people do not believe that you believe what you say you believe.* They may think you're just playing church or practicing an empty religion. They wonder if your faith is just some tradition or religious habit. They are pretty sure you and I don't really believe all this "God stuff."

When we give an authentic and passionate testimony, we declare that we really do believe in a God who is active and powerful. We are not just playing religion. We have encountered the living God and experience him at work in our lives every single day. A well-expressed testimony will communicate to your nonbelieving friends and family members that God is the one who can

- answer prayers,
- heal broken bodies,
- restore shattered hearts,
- put together fragmented marriages,
- set us free from fear and worry,
- release people from addictions,
- wash away sin and remove the cloud of guilt,
- comfort the lonely and hurting, and
- give new purpose and direction in life.

A testimony can be the story of how you came to faith in Jesus and how your life has changed. But more often it's a simple story of something God did in your life recently. It is a declaration that the Jesus who died on the cross to save you is still active in your life right now. This means you don't have one testimony; you have many.

Each week you have new stories to tell of how God is moving and working. When people hear these stories, they are faced with a profound reality. You really do believe what you say you believe—your faith is authentic. The fact that you actually know Jesus and have a dynamic relationship with the God who made you creates interest in hearing more about your spiritual journey and the God you are following.

Helpful Reminders as You Tell Your Story

In some situations your testimony will be a recounting of how you first became a follower of Jesus. At other times it will be a story about how God is at work in your life today. No matter what kind of testimony you share, the following reminders will help you be effective.

1. ASK FOR PERMISSION AND DON'T BE PUSHY

If you have a sense that the door is open to share a testimony, first ask for permission. "Would you mind if I told you a little about a way God has changed my life?" Or, "I'd like to tell you how I first came to have a relationship with Jesus. Would that be all right with you?" We honor people and show them respect when we allow them to tell us whether they are ready to enter into this new level of conversation.

2. USE ORDINARY LANGUAGE

The longer we follow Jesus and the more time we spend with other Christians, the more sensitive we need to be about our language when we tell our story of faith. We can't assume nonbelievers will know what we mean when we refer to sin, redemption, grace, or dozens of other wonderful words. These terms and others like them are rich and helpful when believers are talking together. But when we share a testimony, it is best to assume that others won't know these terms and to use plain language.

I remember one occasion when a young man approached me and tried to witness to me. I was skiing in Lake Tahoe, Nevada, with a group of volunteers from my church. This zealous man talked about the "blood of the Lamb," my need for a "Savior," and the "wages of sin." His heart was in the right place, but his language would have been incomprehensible to most non-Christians. I was a believer when this incident happened, so I eventually let him know that I was "redeemed, sanctified, and justified." Actually, I encouraged him to watch his language so that he could be more effective. He thanked me. As we parted ways I asked him, "Did your group come up here just to witness to people?" He said, "Well, we're skiing in the daytime and fishing at night!"

3. START BRIEFLY AND SHARE MORE AS IT BECOMES APPROPRIATE

A short testimony is almost always better than a long one. Rather than telling your whole life story, try sharing just one experience with God or one event that led you to faith. Then you can always ask, "Could I share a little more about my relationship with Jesus?" This question gives listeners a natural opportunity to enter into the conversation or to let you know that they have heard enough for now. If it looks like a conversation is winding down, make sure they know the door is open to talk at any time.

In his book *Just Walk across the Room*, Bill Hybels encourages believers to develop the discipline of sharing a brief testimony. He suggests trying to share your story in one hundred words or less. One of the churches I serve, Central Wesleyan Church in Holland, Michigan, decided to take this challenge and encouraged the members of the church to give it a try.[42] If you don't think you can capture a compelling story in so few words, read the following examples from people at Central Wesleyan:

> My family always went to church. So when I was young I decided to follow Jesus. Later, I got married and had three children. My life was full and I should have been happy. But I began to feel a deep discontent and unexplainable emptiness. I struggled with suicidal thoughts and feelings of desperation, felt trapped, and wanted to run away. Then a dear friend helped me see what I needed was a relationship with Jesus, not just religion. My life has never been the same. Now when I feel like running, I run to Jesus.
>
> —Tamela

I grew up with no faith. I only heard the name of God when someone slammed a finger in a drawer! Our family focused on being
successful and self-sufficient. The problem was, I wanted purpose
and meaning beyond a good job. Then I heard that living with
faith in Jesus would lead to lasting purpose and meaning. I took a
chance and committed my life to following him. For almost three
decades I have experienced rich purpose in my life. Every day is an
adventure of serving Jesus and loving others. Honestly, I wouldn't
have it any other way.

—Garth

For so long my life was about trying to hold everything together.
Try as I might, my life shattered all around me. I could not put the
pieces together again. Then I finally realized that true faith is more
than saying I believe in Jesus. It's about developing an authentic
relationship with him—loving him with my *whole* heart. I placed
my shattered life in his hands. He took the pieces and lovingly
reshaped them into something beautiful. Now I seek to make a
difference in the lives of others as Christ has for me. Every day is
a gift!

—Mariann

Fifty years before the *Left Behind* books were bestsellers, I was
already thinking about eternal issues. Is there a heaven? Is there
a hell? Where will I spend forever? Desiring to have a hope-filled
eternity, I chose to follow Jesus. I wanted to please God and honor
my family, so I invited Jesus to lead all of my life! I made my
choices—academics, sports, entertainment, education, career, and
marriage—based on my love for God. The result: God has done
what I could not. I experience God's unconditional love as a free
gift every day. And heaven is my eternal destination!

—Wayne

I was arrested for drunkenness and disorderly conduct. The sentence—twenty days in jail. I was only nineteen! My parents were
Christians and I thought their life was boring. My life plan: Have
"lots of fun" now; worry about faith later. While I was in jail,

people were praying for me. Two men from my dad's church came to visit. One said, "You are one heartbeat away from eternity." That night I felt each heartbeat as if it would be my last. I had no peace until I accepted Jesus' forgiveness. Now with every heartbeat I seek to serve God.

—Sherwin

I have always been on a journey of following Jesus. As a boy I asked God to forgive and lead me. I didn't totally know what all this meant, but I was sincere … for a six-year-old. In eighth grade I was growing in my understanding of faith and told God I wanted him to have my whole life. Sadly, I began using drugs and stealing things. I was struggling with peer pressure. Then I switched schools and made new friends, and at winter camp I rededicated my life to following Jesus. I am excited to keep following Jesus; my journey is just beginning!

—Steve (a high school student)

When the door is open to share a testimony, do it with clarity and boldness, but keep it brief. It could lead to questions and deeper discussion, but be careful not to launch into a fifteen-minute story that feels like a sermon!

4. Highlight God's Presence and Power

As you tell your story, make sure God is central. A testimony is not so much about us as it is about the presence and power of the God who is alive in us. One way people will see God in this world is through his power manifested in us.

Some Christians may warn you not to tell "strange and fanciful stories" that will freak people out. I agree. But if God has moved in your life in a powerful way, don't be shy to talk about it. Has Jesus brought you healing? Have you been delivered from an addiction or bad habit? Has the Holy Spirit given you clear leading? All of these stories can be part of your testimony. People want to know if this God you say is real has power to move in this world. If you have seen his power, tell the story.

Testimonies are also about declaring that the presence of Jesus is real. As Christians, we are not playing religion or just going to church events. We have met the living God, the Holy Spirit dwells in us, and Jesus is our closest friend. We can talk with confidence about how we experience the presence of God in our lives, in the hard times and in the good times.

Some years ago, before my brother Jason became a believer, I spent a lot of time with him and hoped he could see that my faith is real. I had already shared the gospel on various occasions, but he hadn't yet responded to the grace of God. In the midst of one conversation, I felt led to share a testimony unlike I had ever shared before. It grew out of my desire for Jason to know that the presence of Jesus in my life is more real than anything.

I asked my brother, "Jason, do you think I'm crazy?"

"What do you mean?" he asked.

"Do you think I'm crazy, nuts, certifiable, that I should be institutionalized?"

He just looked at me, waited, and finally smiled, saying, "You are one of the sanest and most rational people I know."

I replied, "Jason, either Jesus is real, or I am crazy. I want you to know that I talk to him every day, and he answers! Jesus is with me every moment of my day, and he is more real to me than you are. Tomorrow you will get on a plane and fly home to California. I might wonder if you are real, but I will never wonder if Jesus is real." I reinforced my point, saying, "If Jesus is not real and alive today, I should be locked up."

The look on his face assured me that he caught the gravity of what I'd just said.

I did not plan or rehearse this testimony. But I believe it was one more factor in a host of factors that played a part in Jason's journey to Jesus. When people hear us affirm God's power and presence, they know we are serious about our faith. They might not agree with us, but they can't deny our faith is authentic.

5. CLEARLY PRESENT THE BEFORE-AND-AFTER PICTURES

In each of the testimonies at the start of this chapter you can see a clear before-and-after pattern to the story.

- From hate-filled and self-centered relationships to loving and caring relationships.
- From a life without purpose and direction to a life of deep meaning and clear direction.
- From fear of death to confidence in this life and hope for eternity.

Though such a pattern isn't mandatory for every testimony, it does help people see the difference Jesus can make in a life. If you have experienced a transforming work of God, let it become the focus of one of your testimonies. Here are a few more examples:

- From loneliness to a sense of belonging (to God and his family).
- From anxiety to peace.
- From financial irresponsibility and fear to hard work and financial stability.
- From selfishness to generosity.
- From addiction and enslavement to freedom from addictions.

The list of options is as diverse as our life experiences.

6. SHARE THE SOURCE OF LIFE TRANSFORMATION

As we share the story of our life transformation, it is critical that we articulate that Jesus is the source of the change. We could not have brought it about on our own. We don't want our lost friends and family members to think that the transformation in our lives is the result of going to church or hanging out with a nice new group of people or even getting "religious." The only power that can change us from the inside out is the work of Jesus. His death on the cross, in our place, and his resurrection in glory are the reason we are becoming new people. We should be careful to express this as we share our stories.

7. LET JOY SHINE THROUGH

Joy is a universal language. If we talk about God's work in our lives, the amazing changes we are experiencing, and the relationship we have with Jesus, but do so without joy, we will send the wrong message. Knowing the Father, walking with Jesus, and being filled with the Holy Spirit should bring a flow of joy that is visible and contagious.

This is not to say that we should paste on a fake smile and blurt, "Praise the Lord," at the end of every sentence. It means the joy of the Lord is evident in our lives, even in the tough times. When the fruit of the Spirit (Gal. 5:22–23) is growing in our lives, people will see it. Joy is always part of our story, because we know Jesus, the author of joy.

8. COMMUNICATE WITH HUMILITY

A testimony is not a bludgeon we use to pound people into submission. It's a witness to what God is doing in our lives and a gift for others to enjoy. We need to be careful that our testimony does not come across as a speech in which we tell people that we're right and they're wrong, or point out how good we are now and how bad everyone else is who doesn't know Jesus. Rather, a testimony is a humble declaration that God is moving in our lives and that we are grateful for what he is doing.

9. REMEMBER YOU HAVE MANY TESTIMONIES

Be careful not to get locked into one testimony. Don't just memorize a script and robotically deliver the same words with the same inflection every time you tell your story. Instead, listen to the people around you and discover where they are in life. When you share a testimony, make sure it's relevant for them.

For example, if you're talking with someone who is dealing with loneliness and you have experienced God's presence in a way that has strengthened you when you have felt alone, share that testimony. But if you're conversing with a spiritual seeker who is wondering if God provides for our needs and takes care of his people, you might tell a very different story. As you walk with Jesus, you will have more and more stories about how a relationship with God transforms various areas of your life.

People love to hear stories, and that's all a testimony is. In the course of most days you will have opportunities to share organically about the difference your faith in Jesus is making in your life. Pray for these opportunities, notice when the door is open, and then share your stories in natural ways. The Holy Spirit will infuse what you share with power. Remember, your part is not to change lives or even to have all the answers. But you *can* talk about the ways God is moving in your life. Your stories might be just what another person needs to hear.

BEARING KINGDOM FRUIT

Organic Activity: I Can Do That!

- *Try the One Hundred Words Exercise.* Take time to write a personal testimony that is one hundred words or less. You'll be amazed at how short it will be. You might even want to write two or three different brief testimonies. Look at the examples in this chapter to help get you started. Identify an area in which you have experienced personal growth or transformation, and let this shape your testimony. Also, try to capture God's part in the process. Remember, the goal is not to prepare a speech you can memorize. Rather, the point of this exercise is to help you learn to be brief as you tell your stories of faith.
- *Practice Sharing Testimonies.* Sit with a Christian friend or family member and practice sharing a testimony. You might want to tell two or three different stories of how God has worked in your life. Have them use the following checklist to help you develop and sharpen your ability to share testimonies. As you told your stories of God's presence and power:

1. Did you ask permission?
2. Did you use language anyone could understand?
3. Was the testimony too long?
4. What did your listener learn about the presence and power of God?
5. Was there a before-and-after contrast in the story?
6. How did your life change?
7. Was Jesus presented as the one who changes lives?

8. Did you convey a sense of joy while telling your story?

9. Did you exhibit a spirit of humility while communicating?

10. What would your listener suggest to help strengthen this testimony?

Personal Reflection

- Who are three or four spiritually disconnected people I have a relationship with? What area of need or struggle is each one facing? Have I faced a similar situation and experienced God's help as I walked through it? How might my story encourage them or give them hope? (Pray for an opportunity to share a testimony with each of these people.)

- What are some ways God is revealing his power and presence in my life right now? How can these experiences become testimonies in the months to come?

Group Reflection

- Take time to share brief testimonies. Help each other strengthen your ability to share your stories effectively by responding to the evaluation questions in the "Organic Activity" section of this chapter.

- How could a clearly presented testimony impact a person who is not yet a follower of Jesus?

- How might you begin using more testimonies as you interact with spiritual seekers?

Prayer Direction

God of power, you are at work in my life each and every day. You are doing amazing things all the time! Help me notice where you are moving and learn to share these stories with a confident and joy-filled heart.

I also pray that you will tune me in to your presence as I walk through each day. Make our relationship so intimate and rich that when I tell others my story, I sound like I am talking about my closest friend—because I am. Amen.

CHAPTER 13

Sharing Good NEWS

We can love people, pray for them, and serve them, but there comes a time when they need to hear the message of Jesus Christ, the gospel. Every believer can naturally present this simple, clear, and life-changing message.

I am not ashamed of the gospel, because it is the power of God for the salvation of everyone who believes: first for the Jew, then for the Gentile. For in the gospel a righteousness from God is revealed, a righteousness that is by faith from first to last, just as it is written: "The righteous will live by faith."

—Romans 1:16–17

Now, brothers, I want to remind you of the gospel I preached to you, which you received and on which you have taken your stand. By this gospel you are saved, if you hold firmly to the word I preached to you. Otherwise, you have believed in vain.

For what I received I passed on to you as of first importance: that Christ died for our sins according to the Scriptures, that he was buried, that he was raised on the third day according to the Scriptures.

—1 Corinthians 15:1–4

Sometime, someplace, somehow in all the evangelism activities there must be a sharing of faith between the Christian and the non-Christian in such a way that the non-Christian is confronted with the possibility of a faith encounter with Jesus Christ.

—Charles Van Engen,
You Are My Witnesses

Saving faith is found in Jesus alone. In a world of growing pluralism and compromise in some parts of the church, it is helpful to remember the uniqueness of Jesus and the hope that is found exclusively in him. Ajith Fernando, in his book *Sharing the Truth in Love*, makes this point with piercing clarity: "Religious pluralism ... can be held only by rejecting the Christian claim to possess absolute truth. This claim implies that the gospel has the ultimate truth that all people everywhere need to accept. We believe that God has revealed truth to humanity in the Scriptures and supremely in Jesus. This truth is without error and is the only way for the salvation of all peoples all over the world."[43]

And we find this firm conviction expressed over and over again in Scripture.

> Salvation is found in no one else, for there is no other name under heaven given to men by which we must be saved.
>
> —Acts 4:12

> For there is one God and one mediator between God and men, the man Christ Jesus, who gave himself as a ransom for all men—the testimony given in its proper time.
>
> —1 Timothy 2:5–6

> He who has the Son has life; he who does not have the Son of God does not have life.
>
> —1 John 5:12

> Jesus answered, "I am the way and the truth and the life. No one comes to the Father except through me."
>
> —John 14:6

For this faith to permeate communities and nations, followers of Christ must be ready and willing to articulate the *message* of the gospel. We must do more than be good people, feed the poor, care for the earth, and seek justice. All of these are important, but at some point we also need to speak the *words* of life. The apostle Paul puts it this way: "But how can they call on him to save them unless they believe in him? And how can they believe in him if they have never heard about him? And how can they hear about him unless someone tells them? And how will anyone go and tell them without being sent? That is what the Scriptures mean when they say, 'How beautiful are the feet of those who bring good news!' " (Rom. 10:14–15 NLT).

Loving and serving people, living incarnationally, having spiritual conversations, and sharing our testimonies are all important. But there comes a time when believers need to present the message of God's love, the truth of human sin, the hope we find in the sacrifice of Christ, and the call to repent and receive Jesus. We are invited to present the good news to the world. Larry Robertson writes, "The term *gospel* literally and appropriately means 'good news,' since it is a message of hope, speaking to the human condition of sin and promising forgiveness, purpose, and eternal life to those who believe."[44] It is this good news that saves us from our sins, if we receive the gift of grace freely offered by Jesus.

Over the years, I have come to greatly dislike a quote that is quite popular among many Christians. I actually heard two different people recite versions of this quote within four days of writing this chapter. The original quote is attributed to St. Francis of Assisi, but I've heard it phrased in various ways: "Preach the gospel at all times. Use words when necessary."

I understand the spirit of this quote, and I think it makes a good point. But in some cases, people use it as an excuse to avoid articulating their faith.

The truth is that no matter how much we try to live in a way that reveals the presence of Jesus, *words* will still be needed. If I could, I would change the quote to read: "Preach the gospel at all times — and there will *always* be a point when words are necessary." Of course my version is not as pithy or concise, but it is closer to the truth. At some point along the way, everyone needs to hear and comprehend the content of the gospel.

We can present the message of Jesus in many ways, but the basic content remains the same. What follows is a brief walk through the gospel. Take a few minutes to read the section "The Best News Ever" out loud. I've tried to phrase it in the words of a Christian who is speaking to a spiritual seeker who wants to know more about Jesus. You might want to time yourself as you read it. For me, reading this section out loud reminds me that the core of the gospel can be articulated in a matter of minutes.

The Best News Ever

God loves you.

The Bible teaches over and over again that God loves you more than words can express. The whole story of the Bible is filled with this message. The starting point of salvation originated in the heart of God. No matter how you feel about yourself and no matter how others might treat you, God's love is always constant! He longs to be in a close personal relationship with you. He made you, loves you, and cares more about you than you could dream or imagine.

> But you, O Lord, are a compassionate and gracious God,
>   slow to anger, abounding in love and faithfulness.
> —Psalm 86:15

> How great is the love the Father has lavished on us, that we should
> be called children of God! And that is what we are!
> —1 John 3:1

Human beings have broken their relationship with God by sinning.

Sin is the word the Bible uses to describe anything we do that is not consistent with God's perfect plan for our lives. Any wrong thought, any unkind word, any action that hurts others or dishonors God is called "sin." The Bible even teaches that when we know there's something good we should do but fail to do it, we sin. Needless to say, we all sin quite a bit—every day.

Sin destroys our relationship with God. He still loves us, but our sin drives a wedge between us and him. God loves you and wants a restored relationship, but he can't just look the other way and pretend you haven't sinned. Because God is perfectly pure (holy), he can't ignore sin. Because he is perfectly fair (just), he will punish sin. The Bible makes it clear that there is only one punishment for sin. It might sound harsh, but sin demands the death penalty. God's absolute holiness and unparalleled justice demand that this penalty be paid.

This news is the worst news imaginable! Because of our sin, we are all separated from God and condemned to death. This bad news can seem overwhelming—until we realize what God did so that we could have our relationship with him restored.

> All have sinned and fall short of the glory of God.
>
> —Romans 3:23

> For the wages of sin is death, but the gift of God is eternal life in Christ Jesus our Lord.
>
> —Romans 6:23

God did something about this problem, and what he did is the greatest news ever.

Thankfully, God's love is bigger than our sin. Our sin is real, and we are all under the condemnation of death. But God offered to pay the price for us. He came to this earth as a man, Jesus. His birth is what we celebrate at Christmas. Jesus was God in a human body. He lived a real life and experienced real joy, pain, and temptation. He faced the same challenges we face in life. But here's the difference: Jesus never sinned. He did not have one thought, motive, or action that dishonored his Father.

One day Jesus was accused of crimes he didn't commit and was condemned to death. He was stripped, beaten, mocked, and then nailed to a cross and executed as a common criminal. Jesus suffered this brutal death so we wouldn't have to pay the price for our sins. His death was the payment.

Although we have sinned and deserve to die, Jesus sacrificed himself on the cross in our place. His death became ours. He didn't deserve to die. We deserve to die, but we don't have to—if we accept Jesus and enter a relationship with God the Father through him.

The gospel is called the good news because we are offered a pardon for all the wrongs we have ever done and ever will do. We can have new life and a restored relationship with God through Jesus. We don't earn it or deserve it, and we can't take credit for it. All we can do is accept it.

> For God so loved the world that he gave his one and only Son, that whoever believes in him shall not perish but have eternal life.
>
> —John 3:16

> This is love: not that we loved God, but that he loved us and sent his Son as an atoning sacrifice for our sins.
>
> —1 John 4:10

How do we accept Jesus, have our sins washed away, and enter a restored relationship with God?

The Bible tells us that salvation through Jesus is a gift; it is not earned by checking the boxes on some to-do list of good works. The only way we can receive salvation is by placing our faith in Jesus. You can do this by praying and asking Jesus to forgive you and to be the leader of your life. This step of faith means you are admitting your sins to God and telling him you are sorry. It's about asking God to help you live a new and changed life that honors him.

You don't have to know a lot of fancy religious terms. Just tell God that you know you have sinned. Express your sorrow and ask for the forgiveness that comes through the price Jesus paid when he died on the cross for you. Then invite Jesus to enter your life and lead you from this moment on, all the way into eternity. You can put these thoughts in your own words, or you can use this prayer:

Dear God, I need you, maybe more than I have ever known. I admit that I have sinned. I have thought things, said things, and done things that do not please you. [At this point, you might want to be specific with God about some of the sins you are sorry about.] I realize my sins cause me to be under a death sentence. I also have come to know that you sent Jesus, your only Son, to pay the price for my sins by dying in my place on the cross. Jesus, I thank you for giving your life for me. I celebrate that you rose from the dead in victory over sin. I need your forgiveness. Enter my life and become my leader from this moment on. Thank you for all you have done and all you will do in my life. Amen!

When you have lifted up this prayer, you can be confident that you are now in a restored relationship with God and that all of your sins are forgiven.

If we confess our sins, he is faithful and just and will forgive us our sins and purify us from all unrighteousness.

—1 John 1:9

As far as the east is from the west,
   so far has he removed our transgressions from us.
                              —Psalm 103:12

If you confess with your mouth, "Jesus is Lord," and believe in your heart that God raised him from the dead, you will be saved.
                              —Romans 10:9

Life with Jesus is a new beginning!

Making a commitment to follow Jesus is not the end of the road; it is the beginning of a whole new journey with Jesus at the center. Your life will never be the same, and your eternity is secure in Jesus.

Lots of Ways to Tell the Story

There is one gospel but there are many ways to express it. Through the years, I have discovered that different situations call for different articulations of the life-changing message of Jesus. What follows are a few stories that illustrate various ways to communicate the gospel organically.

The five presentations of the good news in the rest of this chapter all come from examples I have learned from leaders like Bill Hybels, Mark Mittelberg, Lee Strobel, James Kennedy, and others who have influenced my understanding of the gospel. Over the years, I've tried to fit as many tools inside my evangelistic toolbox as I possibly can. I am convinced that all Christians should be able to share the message of Jesus in many different ways. For ideas, you may want to check out a classic resource like D. James Kennedy's *Evangelism Explosion*.[45] Or learn how to present the gospel as a response to the law of God with *The Way of the Master* training materials.[46] Another option to consider is the EvangeCube, a big cube that tells the gospel story in pictures. (Great for kids!)

For our purposes, I will focus on just five examples of how the unchanging message of the gospel can be presented in different ways. In each of these examples, I've tried to present a narrative showing how the message of Christ can be expressed to a real person in a real-life situation. You can then pray about how you might reshape each of these approaches to fit your situation. My goal is not to give you a script to memorize but to provide an example you can learn from and personalize. The key is that you begin to get the gospel deep in your heart so you are ready to express it in ways that will connect naturally with those you share it with.

The Record Book

There was a big apartment complex right next to Zion Church. We had an outreach team that followed up on visitors to the church, and we would often drop in just to welcome new families. One evening I stopped by the apartments with another member of the church to welcome two young women who were new to the community.

Cindy and Kathy met us at the door with warm enthusiasm. They were college students who had started moving in the day before, and they seemed quite busy.

We greeted them, invited them to church (it was in their back yard), and asked if they had any questions. They quickly asked if we wanted to come in and talk. We said yes, and they stopped unpacking, sat down, and began asking all kinds of questions about God.

Their eagerness to learn about spiritual things was amazing. Clearly our visit with them was a divine appointment.

After talking for a while and answering a number of their questions, I asked, "Would you mind if I told you how a person can become a follower of Jesus?"

They both seemed interested and said they would love that. I went on to use a simple illustration I had learned from an Evangelism Explosion training program.[47] Over the years, I had changed and adapted it a bit.

I asked if I could borrow a book.

They grabbed one from a box and gave it to me.

I took the book in my hands and said, "Imagine this book contains a record of all the wrongs I have ever done." I flipped slowly through the pages. "It has a chapter on the junior high years, the high school years, and even the college years. Every unkind word, impure thought, and wrong action is recorded in this record book. I'm not an old man, but I don't think this book would be big enough to contain all the wrongs I have done."

They both nodded and listened attentively.

"Well, the Bible says God is perfect and pure. He sees and knows all of our wrongs. Nothing is hidden from him. In his heart is a record book containing every offense we have committed against him, against the people in our lives, and even against ourselves.

"Some days I think I live a pretty good life and the record book of my sins isn't too bad. But then I look at it this way. The Bible teaches that sin is anything we do that is offensive to God—our words, thoughts, actions, even our failure to do good things. Imagine I went through a day when I committed only four sins. I had one bad thought run through my mind—only one all day. I spoke just one thoughtless word. Only one single action in twenty-four hours was out of God's perfect will. And I missed just a single opportunity to be kind, loving, and generous to others. This day would be the best day of my life—I committed just four sins!

"The truth is, if someone cuts me off in traffic, I can sin with my thoughts, words, and actions all in about two seconds. But on this particular day, I sinned just four times."

Cindy and Kathy were listening intently. I could tell they understood that committing only four sins in one day was probably an impossibility for anyone, but they played along.

"Now imagine I live my life with such goodness that I committed just four sins a day, every day, all my life. That would be unheard of, but imagine I live each day with only four sins. If I live to be seventy years old, I would have more than one hundred thousand entries in my record book."

I held the book in my hands and admitted, "I have never lived that good a single day of my life."

They both nodded their heads in agreement as if to say, "Neither have I."

I continued, "The Bible teaches that our sins are what keep us from having a right relationship with God." I held out my left hand, palm upward, and placed the book on my hand, saying, "Each of us has a record book of all the sins and wrongs we have ever committed. These sins are ours. We committed them."

I pointed to my left hand. "This is my life." Then I pointed to the book. "These are my sins. The Bible says that the consequence of my sins is eternal separation from God."

I then lifted my right hand as high as I could and said, "Imagine this is God. I want to get to him, I want a friendship with him, but my sin is always in the way."

I lifted my left hand, with the record book sitting on it, and tried to bring my left and right hands together, but the book was in the way—right between me (my left hand) and God (my right hand).

"The Bible says God loves me and wants to be in a loving relationship with me. But look what stands in the way—my sin." I pointed again at the book.

Kathy and Cindy recognized the dilemma. Even though I was talking about me and my sins, they had made the connection and were thinking about the consequences of their own sins.

"Here's the good news: God loves us so much that he made a commitment to deal with all of our sins. Jesus came to this earth—that's what Christmas is all about—for the express purpose of paying for our sins."

I paraphrased Isaiah 53:6: "We are all like sheep that have wandered away; each of us has decided to do our own thing. But God laid all of our sins and wrongs on Jesus."

I lowered my right hand (representing God) so it was side by side with my left hand and the record book, saying, "Jesus left heaven for you and me, was born on this earth, and never did a single wrong thing. But they put him on a cross, where he died for our sins."

I placed the record book of sins on my right hand (on Jesus) and repeated, "God laid all our sins and wrongs on Jesus."

"When Jesus was hanging on the cross, dying to pay for our sins, one of the things he said was, 'It is finished.' Back in ancient times this term was used in the marketplace when a debt was paid in full. Jesus was saying, 'Through my sacrifice on the cross, all of your debts are paid.'"

I asked Cindy and Kathy, "Where are my sins now?"

They both said, "On Jesus."

"Because I am so good?"

"No!"

"Because I worked hard or went to church?"

"No."

"My salvation came when I accepted Jesus and what he did for me on the cross. It did not come because of any good thing I had ever done. It came as a gift from his loving heart. And I'm now set free to be in relationship with God. My sins are gone."

I asked them if this explanation made sense, and they assured me it did.

I also explained that God has accomplished all that needs to be done for our salvation through Jesus' death on the cross. Our part is to admit we have done wrong, ask for forgiveness, and invite Jesus to enter our lives and lead us from this point on.

I felt led to ask, "Cindy and Kathy, do you want to admit your wrongs and have that record book removed from you so you can have a relationship with God? Are you ready to receive the forgiveness God offers through Jesus?"

Both of them enthusiastically responded yes.

We prayed together, and these two young women passionately asked Jesus to forgive and lead them.

As we finished the prayer and I said, "Amen," Cindy jumped out of her chair, screamed, "Oh no!" and ran out of the room. A moment later we heard another scream and then, "Come here—you have to see this!"

It turns out Cindy had a water bed and had plugged in a hose and started filling it up before we arrived. She had forgotten all about it until we said amen. When we entered her room, we all laughed with her. Her bed looked like a giant water balloon, about three times the size of a normal water bed. Thankfully, it had not exploded.

As we talked about next steps, both Cindy and Kathy told us that they had a bunch of friends who had been trying to get them to visit a church in the area. They committed to contact their friends and begin attending their church. We let them know we were thrilled for them to attend any Bible-believing church and encouraged them to connect with their friends right away. Also, a woman on our team followed up with some resources to help them begin growing in the Word of God, in prayer, and in fellowship. It was a day none of us would ever forget.

The Romans Road

Dante owned a small restaurant, a quiet place where I could study in the afternoons. He was a gregarious guy who loved people and enjoyed cooking. His family had a Catholic background, but he showed very little interest in any kind of personal faith. Over the course of my study times, we developed a friendship.

Once while I was sitting and reading a book, Dante plopped into the seat across from me. Usually this meant we were going to have a nice chat.

"You know how we are Catholic?" he said.

I knew his wife went to church and the kids were attending Catholic school, so I nodded.

"Well, my kids are taking these classes at school where they learn about being Catholic, and sometimes they ask questions I can't answer. Would it be okay if I saved the questions and when you come in we can talk about them?"

I assured him I'd be glad to process these religious questions with him.

Immediately his eyes lit up. "Well then, I have my first question for you."

I started getting excited, but his first question was a tough one.

"Why do we pray to Mary?"

I won't give you my whole answer, but I talked with Dante about how God offers access directly through Jesus. I asked him,

"If you could go to God face-to-face or through someone else, what would you choose?"

"I'd talk to God face-to-face every time," he said.

I admitted that even though it probably wasn't the answer the teachers at the school were looking for, I was convinced that heading to God directly seemed like the best way to communicate with him. I told him, "I don't know much about praying to Mary, saints, or anyone else. But I do know that Jesus makes it possible for us to meet with God and talk to him face-to-face."

Dante's question led to a great conversation about connecting with God. We actually ended up having a Bible study right there in the restaurant—good thing business was slow that day! As we talked, I walked Dante through what has come to be called the "Romans Road," a step-by-step look at some key passages from the book of Romans that present core truths of the faith. This gospel presentation has a few variations, but here are the passages Dante and I read together:

> *Romans 3:23*: "All have sinned and fall short of the glory of God."
>
> *Romans 6:23*: "For the wages of sin is death, but the gift of God is eternal life in Christ Jesus our Lord."
>
> *Romans 10:9–10*: "If you confess with your mouth, 'Jesus is Lord,' and believe in your heart that God raised him from the dead, you will be saved. For it is with your heart that you believe and are justified, and it is with your mouth that you confess and are saved."
>
> *Romans 10:13*: "Everyone who calls on the name of the Lord will be saved."
>
> *Romans 8:1*: "Therefore, there is now no condemnation for those who are in Christ Jesus."
>
> *Romans 12:1–2*: "Therefore, I urge you, brothers, in view of God's mercy, to offer your bodies as living sacrifices, holy and pleasing to God—this is your spiritual act of worship. Do not conform any longer to the pattern of this world, but be transformed by the renewing of your mind. Then you will be able to test and approve what God's will is—his good, pleasing and perfect will."

Notice that I didn't quote these verses from memory or give Dante a sermon; I actually just had these passages highlighted in my Bible. We discussed them one at a time and even took turns reading them. Dante thought that was pretty cool. I don't think he had read much from the Bible before. With each passage we read, Dante had questions. He also felt free to tell me what he thought the passage was saying.

This gospel presentation came in the form of a discussion between two friends. We looked at what the Bible said and reflected on it together. I was amazed by Dante's insights and his hunger to learn. This moment became just one among many in which we would talk about faith. Each time we talked, Dante had an opportunity to get a clearer picture of the good news of Jesus.

Do versus Done

I learned the "Do versus Done" presentation of the gospel when I first went through the *Contagious Christian* training.[48] Over the following seven or eight years, I taught the Becoming a Contagious Christian class at my church at least twice a year. This curriculum teaches some solid gospel presentations and is an amazing tool to help people discover their outreach style.

One time I was in line at a Subway sandwich shop when the young woman behind the counter began chatting with me as she made my meatball sub.

"What kind of bread would you like?"

"Let's go with wheat."

As she cut the bread, she asked me, "So what do you do?"

"I'm a pastor in town here. The church is only about seven minutes from here."

She glanced up and took a good look at me. "You don't seem like the religious type," she said. Then she asked if I wanted cheese on my sub.

I asked her, "What does a religious type look like?"

"I don't know exactly, but you don't look the type."

I thanked her for observing that I did not look religious (because I sensed in her tone that being religious was not a good thing in her mind). Then I asked for provolone cheese and told her, "I don't consider myself religious, but I am a Christian."

She looked at me quizzically, and I could tell she was trying to sort out what I meant, so I asked, "Would you like me to explain the difference between being religious and being a Christian?"

She said, "Yes, and what kind of veggies would you like?"

As we moved down the sandwich assembly line, I told her what to put on my sub and also shared a simple presentation of the gospel.

"Being religious is spelled DO, and being a Christian is spelled DONE. For most people religion is about what they *do*. Do you go to church? Do you give money? Do you follow the rules? Do you live a good life? This bases the whole thing on our actions—what we *do*.

"Christianity is radically different. It's all about what God has *done*. God loved us and sent Jesus into the world—that's Christmas. Jesus lived a perfect life, but he was still killed on a cross, and three days later he rose again from the dead—that's Easter. God offers to clean up all the messes we have made in our lives and invites us into his family through faith in his Son, Jesus. God has *done* it all. Our part is just to receive the free gift he offers."

By this point the veggies were on my sub and she was wrapping it up.

"Do you want to make this a meal deal?" she asked.

I told her the sandwich was all I needed that day, and as we stood at the register, I said, "You know, my life is not about religion and following a big heavenly to-do list. I'm all about what Jesus has *done* for me. I'm not very religious, but I am a Christian."

Then I asked her, "Did my explanation make sense?"

She said it was actually quite helpful.

I paid for my sub, thanked her for the conversation, and said, "I'll be here for an occasional sandwich, and we can talk more if you like."

She said she would enjoy that.

The ABCs of Salvation

I had a chance to spend a week volunteering as a counselor for a group of third-grade boys at a week-long summer Bible club. It was an amazing time. Some of the boys came from a home with a church background, but a number of them were starting with a blank slate—they had never been to church.

On the first day we talked about prayer, and even the non-churched kids got into the spirit of things. The boys shared prayer needs with each other and prayed with passion. The kids with no faith background were willing to pray out loud and ask for God's help for each other as well as lifting up prayers of thanks. One boy had a sick turtle, and the others rallied around him in prayer. Each morning they would ask how his turtle was feeling as we spent time in prayer. It was a joy!

Throughout the week we played all kinds of games, sang songs, did craft projects, prayed, and had Bible studies. As the final day of the Bible club approached, I prayed about how I might present the gospel in a way the boys would understand and remember. I decided to use a little tool called the ABCs of salvation. Though there are many versions of this, I explained it to the guys this way:

"There's a very simple way to understand the message of Jesus. It's called the ABCs of salvation because the main ideas start with the letters A, B, and C.

"The A is to *accept* Jesus as the one who will lead your life. All of us like to do whatever we want, but the best way to live is to follow Jesus' plan for us."

I held up my Bible and explained that God gave us this book to help us know how to be kind to each other, how to live for him, how to make smart decisions, what to stay away from, and lots of other things that will help us know how to live.

I continued, "Becoming a Christian means we accept that God is way smarter than we are and he knows what is best for us. So when we accept Jesus, we agree to do our best to follow his plan and his ways."

They listened—as well as a group of third-grade boys can.

"The B is to *believe* what the Bible says about Jesus. It teaches us that he was God in a human body. He came to earth from heaven, and that's why we celebrate Christmas. He also lived a perfect life and never did a single wrong thing. But people still treated him badly and ended up killing him. The Bible teaches us that after three days in the grave, Jesus came back to life. Jesus is still alive today and loves each one of us. It's important that we believe Jesus is who he said he is.

"The C is to *confess* the wrong things you have done and ask God to forgive you. First, we accept Jesus as the leader of our lives. Then we believe he is the one who came from heaven to pay for all our wrongs by giving his life for us. But there's one more thing we must do. We need to tell God we are sorry for all our wrongs. All of us have said mean things, hurt others' feelings, done things that are wrong, and thought bad thoughts."

The boys all nodded their heads as I talked about doing wrong things.

"The Bible says we need to confess our sins. That's just a fancy way of saying we need to tell God we are truly sorry for the wrongs we have done. When we do this, God washes away all our wrongs and gives us a fresh new start."

I asked the boys, "Have any of you already come to a point in your life when you have *accepted* Jesus, *believed* in him, and *confessed* your sins?"

About a third of them raised their hands or nodded their heads.

Then I asked, "Would anyone like to follow the ABCs of salvation today and accept Jesus, tell him you believe, and confess your sins?"

Several of the boys were ready to take this step, and we had a wonderful time of prayer and celebration. I also talked with the whole group about how those who didn't feel ready at that moment could accept, believe, and confess anytime and anywhere.

The Bridge of Life

I met Gerome through Rosie, a woman in our church. She worked with him, and he had grown to be open to spiritual things. They had lots of conversations, but she felt it would be healthy to have a Christian man connect with Gerome and asked if I would be willing to meet with him.

What followed was the development of a friendship and a pattern of meeting for coffee and conversation about once a month. Gerome was curious and open, but I found out that he was also dealing with many questions and some serious roadblocks when it came to faith in Jesus. At one point Gerome said, "I'm pretty sure I'm going to become a Christian, but I just don't know when."

His comment was both hopeful and a reminder that he was still working through some issues. I never tried to force Gerome to make a commitment, but I asked him on numerous occasions, "Do you think you are at a place where you are ready to surrender your life to Jesus and commit to be his follower?" Each time he had a reason to wait. So I waited with him and we kept meeting and talking about life and faith.

One time we were in a local coffee shop and I was trying to help Gerome get a clearer picture of the gospel. I was also trying to get an assessment of where he was on his spiritual journey. I took out a piece of paper and began drawing a picture. By this point Gerome had gained a fair amount of spiritual information; he had even been reading the Bible and was seeking diligently. In his case, I knew I could use some language I would not have used with a person who was in the beginning of their spiritual journey. What I drew was a simple illustration I had learned many years before, had taught in the Becoming a Contagious Christian course, and had also seen recently in Bill Hybels's book *Just Walk across the Room*. It's a tool used by people in many different situations and cultures to share the gospel of Jesus.

I am not an artist by any stretch of the imagination, but the simple images seemed to help me explain the gospel to Gerome. First I drew this:

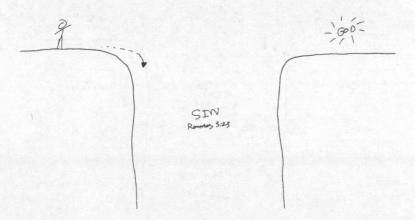

I said, "Gerome, we've had lots of conversations over the past months about what the Bible says and what we each believe. This picture is a simple way to portray what the Bible teaches about human beings and God. Even though God loves us, we are separated from him because of our sins. Romans 3:23 says, 'All have sinned and fall short of the glory of God.' That's what this picture represents. Sin is this giant chasm between us and God. God does not like it, he does not want it, but that is what sin does. It separates us from God."

I asked Gerome if he had ever been to the Grand Canyon. He told me he had and shared a bit about his trip out west.

I said, "Since you have seen the Grand Canyon, I want you to imagine that it's the chasm in this little drawing. The Grand Canyon separates you from God. The truth is this chasm is even bigger, but a mental image of the Grand Canyon will give you a sense of the problem. Now, imagine you are on one side and God is on the other. How will you get across? What if you ran as fast as you could and jumped for the other side? What would happen?"

Gerome laughed and said, "Splat!"

"What if the best long jumper in the world tried to run and jump the Grand Canyon?"

Again, "Splat."

I agreed and added to the drawing as I made some spiritual connections in the story.

236

"Imagine the person on this side of the canyon is you. You want to get to God, so you try as hard as you can. You do some good works and nice things hoping these gestures will be enough to span the distance between you and God. But trying to do enough good things is a lot like trying to jump the Grand Canyon—the distance is too far. Even someone who spends their whole life training and seeking to be good can't make it across in their own strength."

I drew more people into the picture on the left side of the chasm, and as I talked about how we might try to do good things to span the distance to God, I drew an arrow representing people jumping off the edge trying to get to God. Then I drew another arrow as I spoke of people who might spend their whole lives trying to be good enough. They might get farther out before gravity takes over, but the weight of sin always wins and everyone ends up on the bottom of the canyon floor.

I wrote the word "death" in the middle of the chasm and shared the first part of Romans 6:23: "For the wages of sin is death."

"The Bible teaches exactly what you said earlier. There's a big spiritual splat every time we try to get to God in our own strength. The distance is too far. We can't do enough good things. We don't have the strength. So the result ends up the same every time—death."

Because I knew where Gerome was in his spiritual journey, I had no question as to whether this truth was hard for him to hear. But it was important to walk through the basic message of the gospel. Sin does separate us from God, and we are all sinners. There's no way we can get to God in our own strength or by our works. But I then moved quickly to the good news.

"I know this reality is upsetting, but the one who is most concerned about our spiritual condition is God. He grieves over our separation so much, and loves us so intensely, that he made a way to span the chasm of sin. He built a bridge to bring us to himself. The Bible says, 'For God so loved the world that he gave his one and only Son, that whoever believes in him shall not perish but have eternal life' (John 3:16). I call this the football verse because at NFL games there always seems to be some guy in the end zone holding up a sign with 'John 3:16' written on it. This little passage in the Bible captures the most amazing truth in the history of the world. God loved you and me so much that he actually allowed his only Son, Jesus, to come to this earth to live, to be crucified, and to die for our sins."

I drew on the sheet some more.

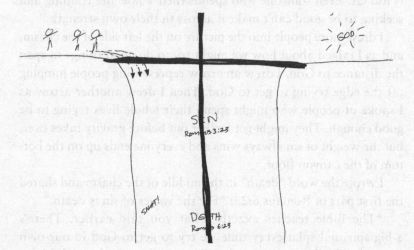

I wrote "John 3:16" above God and then began talking about what God has done to deal with the chasm of sin and death. I said, "When God sent his Son, Jesus, into the world, he had a specific mission. He came to deal with our sin and offer us new life. That's why he died on the cross. When Jesus was on the cross, he was paying the price for our sins—for yours and mine. He knew each of us by name and all the wrongs we have ever done, and he came to pay the price!"

I drew a bold vertical line down the center of the page, right through the words "sin" and "death." Then I drew a horizontal line bridging the gap between people and God. These two lines form a cross, the bridge over sin.

I said to Gerome, "That's the basic story of God and people. God loves us, sin separates us, and Jesus has made a way for us to cross over and be in a restored relationship with the Father."

I asked him, "Where do you see yourself in this picture right now?"

Before Gerome could answer, I experienced one of my funniest outreach moments to date. A pastor friend of mine came walking up to our table and said to Gerome, "Hey, don't believe a word this guy says," as he pointed at me. "Whatever he's trying to sell, don't buy it!"

Of course he was joking, but as he stepped up to the table, he saw the piece of paper and the bridge illustration. His face turned bright red, and he apologized and slowly backed away, saying, "I was just kidding—sorry." We still laugh about it today.

Gerome realized this guy was a buddy of mine and was just messing around, and we got back to our conversation. He looked at the diagram and pointed at the very edge of the left side of the cross. "I'm right there, ready to walk across and meet God."

Crossing the Line of Faith

Just as there is a need to clearly communicate the content of the gospel, there is also a time to ask people if they are ready to take that step and cross the line of faith. We don't force this decision on others or coerce people into accepting Christ. But we *can* extend an invitation.

As Gerome pointed to the diagram it was clear he was as close as possible but had not crossed over. I asked him, "Are you ready to take that step and receive what Jesus has done for you? Are you at the point where you are ready to confess your sin and embrace Jesus?"

I wish I could say he said yes, but he still had some reservations. We chatted a bit more, set another date to meet, and said goodbye. As I drove off, I cried out to God. "Lord, work in Gerome's heart, break down his resistance, and bring him to yourself." About a week later I got a call—Gerome had received Jesus! I found out that he had attended church with a friend, and during an invitation, he publicly responded to the offer of salvation in Christ. I joined the angels in heaven as I rejoiced over his new life in Christ.

As we walk with people toward Jesus, there will be times when we feel prompted to ask if they are ready to pray and receive him as Savior and Lord. In these moments, be gentle and bold. Extend the invitation. If they are *not* ready, don't lose heart—be patient and press on. If they *are* ready, lead them through a simple prayer. Ask the person to pray each line of the prayer after you. Try to read each line slowly—don't rush it. If you aren't sure what to say, you could use this sample prayer:

> *Dear God, I need you.*
> *I admit that I have sinned.*
> *I have thought things,*
> *said things,*
> *and done things,*
> *that do not please you.*
> *I confess my sins.*
> *I believe you sent Jesus,*
> *your only Son,*
> *to pay the price for my sins*
> *by dying in my place*
> *on the cross.*
> *Jesus, I thank you*
> *for giving your life for me.*
> *Thank you for the cross.*
> *Thank you for your resurrection.*
> *I need your forgiveness.*
> *Enter my life,*
> *and be my leader from this moment on.*
> *Thank you for all you have done*
> *and all you will do in my life.*
> *Amen!*

At the end of the prayer, feel free to lift up your own prayer of thanks for the commitment your friend has just made. If you decide to do this, simply keep praying but increase your pace a little bit so it is clear they are no longer repeating after you. Here are some ideas of what to pray for:

- Thank God for their commitment.
- Ask the Holy Spirit to guide their future.

- Pray for them to have confidence and assurance that they are now a child of God.
- Ask for the Spirit's protection on their life as they resist temptation and turn away from past sinful patterns.
- Pray for them to grow in maturity and learn to walk as a follower of Jesus.

After you have prayed, you can focus on next steps. Once people have made a commitment to follow Jesus, the adventure is just beginning. As the person who walked with them on their spiritual journey up to this point, you can help as they press forward in growing up in faith. I can't begin to plumb the depths of all that is involved in discipleship, but we must never forget that evangelism and discipleship go hand in hand. Jesus told us to "go and make disciples of all nations, baptizing them in the name of the Father and of the Son and of the Holy Spirit, and teaching them to obey everything I have commanded you" (Matt. 28:19–20). We are not just called to make converts and get people baptized; we are commanded to teach people how to be disciples of Jesus.

If you follow God's plan for your life and engage in organic outreach, it is critical that you grow in your ability to help new believers move toward maturity. Four books that provide a solid starting place are *Celebration of Discipline* by Richard Foster, *The Life You've Always Wanted* by John Ortberg (the expanded edition has discussion questions and life-application ideas that I was able to write and develop for John), *The Pursuit of Holiness* by Jerry Bridges, and *Seismic Shifts*, a book I wrote.[49]

The issue is not so much what books or resources you use, but that you help new believers grow in their faith and take the next steps in their journey with Jesus. These steps include growing in personal study of the Scriptures, learning to pray with passion, connecting in community with other believers, finding their spiritual gifts and place of service, sharing their newfound faith organically, and so much more. God invites us into the adventure of helping new believers grow up in faith.

Stay Open to the Spirit

As you finish this book, I'm convinced that the Holy Spirit is ready to launch you into new places of faithfulness and fruitfulness as you engage in organic outreach. Keep your eyes open: God will show you doors to enter. Listen closely for the whisper of the Spirit. Serve humbly in the name of Jesus. Pray daily for opportunities to share God's love. Study diligently so the Word of God is alive in your heart and mind. And always be ready to tell the life-changing story of the gospel.

You do your part, and God will do his. Then when the harvest comes in, God gets the glory and you get to join the party—and what a celebration it will be!

BEARING KINGDOM FRUIT

Organic Activity: I Can Do That!

- *Practice a Presentation.* Choose one of the sample gospel presentations in this chapter and practice it. But don't do this in a vacuum. Imagine you are sharing the message with a specific person you know who is not yet a follower of Jesus. After you practice, pray that God will open the door for you to share this good news face-to-face.

Personal Reflection

- Which of these presentations would feel most natural if I had an opportunity to share the gospel with a specific person in my life?
- What two or three presentations of the gospel feel most natural to me?

Group Reflection

- Tell about a time you shared the gospel using one of these approaches.
- Tell about a time you shared the message of Jesus using another approach or presentation.
- Why is it valuable to be able to share the gospel in a variety of ways?

Prayer Direction

Here I am, Lord. I have received your good news and it has changed my life. Your love and presence are still transforming me every day. Now I am ready to go out into the harvest fields of this world and be part of your plan to bring your good news everywhere. Give me boldness. Grant me humility. Help me to be ever ready to tell others about the hope you have unleashed in my life. Use me, Lord, to be salt and light today and every day. Amen!

Notes

1. The focus of this book is on helping Christians share their faith naturally. Even the teaching sections are narrative and are intended to present outreach as something that happens in the natural flow of life.

2. When the apostle Paul was in prison for preaching the gospel, people were actually doing evangelism so they could irritate him. Their motives were wrong, but Paul still declared that God could use their efforts. Our motive should be love, but God is big enough to use imperfect motives to accomplish his purposes.

3. Ajith Fernando, in *Sharing the Truth in Love: How to Relate to People of Other Faiths* (Grand Rapids: Discovery House, 2001), does an outstanding job of clarifying the connections between what we believe and how our beliefs impact our outreach. Fernando is a leader in the church in Sri Lanka and ministers all over the world. I commend his books to all who love God's Word and have a passion for learning biblical truth.

4. Thom Rainer, *Surprising Insights from the Unchurched and Proven Ways to Reach Them* (Grand Rapids: Zondervan, 2001). If you appreciate solid research and thoughtful analysis, take time to read any of Rainer's books. You will learn and be inspired.

5. Ibid., 130.

6. In *The Lost Message of Jesus* (Grand Rapids: Zondervan, 2004), 182–83, Steve Chalke and Alan Mann describe penal substitution as "a form of cosmic child abuse" that "makes a mockery of Jesus' own teaching to love your enemies." In *Why We're Not Emergent (By Two Guys Who Should Be)* (Chicago: Moody, 2008), 192–94, Kevin DeYoung and Ted Kluck unpack this development in greater detail. A growing number of pastors and authors seem embarrassed by the idea that Jesus died in our place and for our sins.

7. Pluralism is the idea that all religions are equally valid. Universalism is the teaching that everyone will go to heaven, no

matter what they believe or how they live. These ideas are becoming more popular even among those who call themselves Bible-believing Christians.

8. Many books look closely at the uniqueness of the Christian faith among the religions of the world. For a thoughtful treatment of this topic, see Fernando, *Sharing the Truth in Love*, and Ravi Zacharias, *Jesus among Other Gods: The Absolute Claims of the Christian Message* (Nashville: Thomas Nelson, 2002).

9. Fernando, *Sharing the Truth in Love*, 185.

10. Rob Bell, *Velvet Elvis* (Grand Rapids: Zondervan, 2006), 21. On the back cover of the book, Bell invites the reader to test and probe what he has written, saying, "Don't swallow it uncritically. Think about it. Wrestle with it." That's what I am doing in my response to some of the content in his book.

11. DeYoung and Kluck, *Why We're Not Emergent*, 196. I've known Kevin DeYoung for many years and respect him as a pastor and scholar. In *Why We're Not Emergent*, he and Kluck have done excellent research and a solid job of evaluating the beliefs of emergent leaders. Their book provides a window to where some leaders are seeking to take the church.

12. Floyd Schneider, "The Scriptures," in *The Complete Evangelism Guidebook: Expert Advice on Reaching Others for Christ*, ed. Scott Dawson (Grand Rapids: Baker, 2006), 76.

13. Penn Jillette, "Penn Says: A Gift of a Bible," http://www.youtube.com/watch?v=7JHS8adO3hM, accessed March 2009, emphasis added.

14. Bill Hybels, with Kevin G. Harney and Sherry Harney, *Reaching Out: Sharing God's Love Naturally* (Grand Rapids: Zondervan, 2005) is a practical, six-week small group study on the topic of personal evangelism.

15. A dear friend of mine, Gary Thomas, has written a wonderful book titled *The Beautiful Fight: Surrendering to the Transforming Presence of God Every Day of Your Life* (Grand Rapids: Zondervan, 2007). In this book he tells a similar story. As strange as it may seem, we both experienced God's touch in almost the same way!

16. Joe Aldrich, *Lifestyle Evangelism: Learning to Open Your Life to Those around You* (Sisters, Ore.: Multnomah, 1981).

17. Ibid., 15.

18. Bill Hybels and Mark Mittelberg, *Becoming a Contagious Christian* (Grand Rapids: Zondervan, 1996).

19. Aldrich, *Lifestyle Evangelism*, 84–85. This book is a classic on relational outreach.

20. This image has been popularized in a short film titled *Bullhorn* by Rob Bell (Nooma 9 [Grand Rapids: Zondervan, 2005]). I don't believe the intention of this film is to discourage evangelism; I think the intention is exactly the opposite. But holding up this caricature as a negative example and urging people not to be like this can have the effect of discouraging people from reaching out.

21. For more information about Faith Church, visit www.faith churchonline.org.

22. R. A. Torrey and E. M. Bounds are two of the classic writers on prayer. Reading any of their work would be a blessing.

23. Josh Fox and Dan Kimball pastor this church. It is a powerful example of an incarnational ministry that teaches the truth of God's Word in ways that fit the culture of the people in the community. For more information on Vintage Faith, check out www.vintagechurch.org.

24. Charles Van Engen, *You Are My Witnesses: Drawing from Your Spiritual Journey to Evangelize Your Neighbors* (New York: Reformed Church Press, 1992). Dr. Van Engen has taught missions at Fuller Theological Seminary for about two decades. He understands evangelism and missions both in the United States and in other cultures. Anything he has written on outreach or missions is worth a read.

25. Since this website is secular in nature, there can be some raw comments and images. The postcards that people send in reveal a depth of pain and hurt that must break the heart of God.

26. Marilyn Hontz, *Listening for God* (Wheaton, Ill.: Tyndale, 2004), 188.

27. Randy Frazee, *Making Room for Life: Trading Chaotic Lifestyles for Connected Relationships* (Grand Rapids: Zondervan,

2003), provides many ideas for doing natural outreach and connecting with people in your neighborhood. This book challenges believers of all walks to make space for going deeper with neighbors.

28. Thomas, *The Beautiful Fight*, 207.

29. Rebecca Manley Pippert, *Out of the Saltshaker and into the World*, rev. and expanded (Downers Grove, Ill.: InterVarsity, 1999), 35. This book is still one of the best introductions to personal evangelism ever written.

30. My book *Seismic Shifts: The Little Changes That Make a Big Difference in Your Life* (2005; repr., Grand Rapids: Zondervan, 2009) covers many topics and includes three chapters on joy and three on personal evangelism. For more information, see www.seismicshifts.com.

31. The point Kennedy makes is an important one. Many of the people who criticize various outreach efforts do very little in terms of personal evangelism. Kennedy is saying, "At least I'm trying something!"

32. I first read about this concept in the *Contagious Christian* materials developed by the Willow Creek Association. To learn more about these outreach resources and other ministry tools, visit www.willowcreek.com.

33. Over the years, after I've shared my testimony with church people, some have come up to me and argued that it was wrong for the church youth group to sponsor a casino night. I don't agree or disagree with them; I simply say, "That's what they did, and it connected for me."

34. Robert E. Coleman, *The Master Plan of Evangelism* (Old Tappan, NJ: Revell, 1963), 66. This book is a classic that should be read by all who are passionate about organic outreach.

35. James F. Engel and Wilbert Norton, *What's Gone Wrong with the Harvest? A Communication Strategy for the Church and World Evangelism* (Grand Rapids: Zondervan, 1975), 45.

36. Using a scale to identify where people are in their spiritual journeys might not seem organic at first glance. The point of using this example, and that of Thom Rainer, is not to encourage the

use of a scale or system. The point is that we recognize that nonbelievers can be in radically different places in their openness to faith and spiritual conversations. This awareness allows us to be more organic as we interact with our unbelieving family members and friends.

37. Thom Rainer, *The Unchurched Next Door: Understanding Faith Stages as Keys to Sharing Your Faith* (Grand Rapids: Zondervan, 2008).

38. Ibid., 21.

39. Lee Strobel, *The Case for Faith: A Journalist Investigates the Toughest Objections to Christianity* (Grand Rapids: Zondervan, 2000). In this book and in *The Case for Christ: A Journalist's Personal Investigation of the Evidence for Jesus* (Grand Rapids: Zondervan, 1998), Strobel does a fantastic job of answering many of the questions spiritually curious people are asking.

40. Mark Mittelberg, *Choosing Your Faith in a World of Spiritual Options* (Wheaton, Ill.: Tyndale, 2008), walks people through many complex questions and challenges relating to the pluralism that exists in our world today. Mittelberg helps readers forward on a journey that allows them to discover the beauty and truth of the Christian faith as they reflect on the various pathways offered by other religions. For more information, visit www.choosingyourfaith.com.

41. Jay Strack, "Welcome Common Questions," in *The Complete Evangelism Guidebook,* 82.

42. Central Wesleyan Church (www.centralwesleyan.org) has a dynamic outreach ministry. The lead pastor, Paul Hontz, has set a goal to have every ministry in the church focused on outreach. This goal is expressed in the statement "Our mission is to become fully devoted followers of Christ as we build redemptive bridges of influence to reach Holland and beyond."

43. Fernando, *Sharing the Truth in Love*, 15.

44. Larry D. Robertson, "Gospel Presentation," in *The Complete Evangelism Guidebook*, 70.

45. D. James Kennedy, *Evangelism Explosion*, 4th ed. (Wheaton, Ill.: Tyndale, 1996).

46. Kirk Cameron and Ray Comfort, *The Way of the Master: Basic Training Course*, DVD (Bartlesville, Okla.: Genesis, 2006).
47. Evangelism Explosion (or EE) is an extensive training program for personal and churchwide evangelism. For more information, visit www.eeinternational.org.
48. Mark Mittelberg, Lee Strobel, and Bill Hybels, *Becoming a Contagious Christian*, DVD (Grand Rapids: Zondervan, 2003).
49. Richard J. Foster, *Celebration of Discipline: The Path to Spiritual Growth* (New York: HarperOne, 1998); John Ortberg, *The Life You've Always Wanted*, expanded ed. (Grand Rapids: Zondervan, 2002); Jerry Bridges, *The Pursuit of Holiness* (Colorado Springs: NAVPress, 2006); Kevin G. Harney, *Seismic Shifts: The Little Changes That Make a Big Difference in Your Life* (2005; repr., Grand Rapids: Zondervan, 2009).

Recommended Resources

Books to Give Spiritual Seekers

Eldredge, John. *Epic: The Story God Is Telling.* Nashville: Thomas Nelson, 2007.

Keller, Timothy. *The Reason for God: Belief in an Age of Skepticism.* New York: Dutton, 2008.

Kimball, Dan. *They Like Jesus but Not the Church: Insights from Emerging Generations.* Grand Rapids: Zondervan, 2007.

Lewis, C. S. The Chronicles of Narnia. 7 vols. New York: HarperCollins, 2005.

Lewis, C. S. *Mere Christianity.* New York: HarperOne, 2001.

Lucado, Max. *He Did This Just for You.* Nashville: Thomas Nelson, 2005.

McDowell, Josh. *More Than a Carpenter.* Wheaton, Ill.: Living Books, 1977.

Mittelberg, Mark. *Choosing Your Faith in a World of Spiritual Options.* Wheaton, Ill.: Tyndale, 2008.

Stanley, Andy. *The Best Question Ever: Learning to Foolproof Your Life.* Sisters, Ore.: Multnomah, 2004.

Stott, John R. W. *Basic Christianity.* IVP Classics. Downers Grove, Ill.: InterVarsity, 2007.

Stott, John R. W. *Becoming a Christian.* Downers Grove, Ill.: InterVarsity, 1999.

Strobel, Lee. *The Case for Christ: A Journalist's Personal Investigation of the Evidence for Jesus.* Grand Rapids: Zondervan, 1998.

Strobel, Lee. *The Case for a Creator: A Journalist Investigates Specific Evidence That Points toward God.* Grand Rapids: Zondervan, 2005.

Strobel, Lee. *The Case for Faith: A Journalist Investigates the Toughest Objections to Christianity*. Grand Rapids: Zondervan, 2000.

Strobel, Lee. *The Case for the Real Jesus: A Journalist Investigates Current Attacks on the Identity of Christ*. Grand Rapids: Zondervan, 2009.

Yancey, Philip. *The Jesus I Never Knew*. Grand Rapids: Zondervan, 2002.

Bibles for the Spiritually Disconnected

Choosing Your Faith New Testament. New Living Translation. With notes from Mark Mittelberg. Wheaton, Ill.: Tyndale, 2008.

The Journey: A Bible for the Spiritually Curious. New International Version. Grand Rapids: Zondervan, 1999.

NIV Quest Study Bible. Rev. ed. Grand Rapids: Zondervan, 2003.

Helpful Websites

www.alpharesources.org/index.cfm
www.billygraham.org/SH_StepstoPeace.asp
www.billygraham.org/SpiritualHelp_Index.asp
www.borderlandsweb.com
www.harvest.org/knowgod/
www.jesuscentral.com
www.leestrobel.com

Study Guides for Seeker Small Groups

Ashton, Mark. Reality Check Series. Grand Rapids: Zondervan, 2002.

Hybels, Bill, with Kevin G. Harney and Sherry Harney. *Reaching Out: Sharing God's Love Naturally*. Grand Rapids: Zondervan, 2005.

Mittelberg, Mark. *Choosing Your Faith Study Guide*. Wheaton, Ill.: Tyndale, 2009.

Poole, Garry. Tough Questions Series. Grand Rapids: Zondervan, 2003.

Richardson, Rick. Groups Investigating God Series. Downers Grove, Ill.: InterVarsity, 2002.

Evangelism Training Courses

Hybels, Bill. *Just Walk across the Room: Simple Steps Pointing People to Faith*. Grand Rapids: Zondervan, 2006.

Mittelberg, Mark. *Becoming a Contagious Church: Increasing Your Church's Evangelistic Temperature*. Grand Rapids: Zondervan, 2007.

Mittelberg, Mark, Lee Strobel, and Bill Hybels. *Becoming a Contagious Christian*. DVD. Grand Rapids: Zondervan, 2006. Six-session course for seminars and small groups.

Poole, Garry. *Seeker Small Groups: Engaging Spiritual Seekers in Life-Changing Discussions*. Grand Rapids: Zondervan, 2003.

Tactics

A Game Plan for Discussing Your Christian Convictions

Author: Gregory Koukl

In a world increasingly indifferent to Christian truth, followers of Christ need to be equipped to communicate with those who do not speak their language or accept their source of authority. Gregory Koukl demonstrates how to get in the driver's seat, keeping any conversation moving with thoughtful, artful diplomacy.

You'll learn how to maneuver comfortably and graciously through the minefields, stop challengers in their tracks, turn the tables and—most importantly—get people thinking about Jesus. Soon, your conversations will look more like diplomacy than D-Day.

Drawing on extensive experience defending Christianity in the public square, Koukl shows you how to:

- Present the truth clearly, cleverly, and persuasively
- Graciously and effectively expose faulty thinking
- Skillfully manage the details of dialogue
- Maintain an engaging, disarming style even under attack

Tactics provides the game plan for communicating the compelling truth about Christianity with confidence and grace.

Softcover: 978-0-310-28292-1

Seismic Shifts

The Little Changes That Make a Big Difference in Your Life

Author: Kevin G. Harney

It's easy to talk about changing your life.
Here's how to actually do it.
Just as seismic shifts in the natural world have radical and far-reaching effects, there are seismic shifts in our personal lives that can transform our hearts, relationships, physical health, faith, and every aspect of our lives. These are the little changes that can make the big difference!

> Small changes can yield huge transformations in the most important areas of your life. My friend Kevin Harney shows you how in his inspiring and practical book.
>
> —Lee Strobel, author,
> *The Case for Christ* and
> *The Case for a Creator*

> Kevin Harney is both a gifted communicator and a seasoned pastor. *Seismic Shifts* will be a gift to individuals and churches alike.
>
> —John Ortberg, author,
> *God Is Closer Than You Think* and
> *The Life You've Always Wanted*

> Kevin Harney is totally on track with *Seismic Shifts*. With skillful pen, Kevin teaches us how to create powerful movement in our lives.
>
> —Randy Frazee, Teaching Pastor
> at Willow Creek Community Church;
> author, *Making Room for Life*

Now in Softcover! 978-0-310-29158-9

ZONDERVAN®
.com

Share Your Thoughts

With the Author: Your comments will be forwarded to
the author when you send them to *zauthor@zondervan.com*.

With Zondervan: Submit your review of this book
by writing to *zreview@zondervan.com*.

Free Online Resources at
www.zondervan.com

Zondervan AuthorTracker: Be notified whenever your
favorite authors publish new books, go on tour, or post
an update about what's happening in their lives.

Daily Bible Verses and Devotions: Enrich your life
with daily Bible verses or devotions that help you start
every morning focused on God.

Free Email Publications: Sign up for newsletters on
fiction, Christian living, church ministry, parenting, and
more.

Zondervan Bible Search: Find and compare
Bible passages in a variety of translations at
www.zondervanbiblesearch.com.

Other Benefits: Register yourself to receive online
benefits like coupons and special offers, or to participate
in research.